DEVLIN DONALDSON AND STEVE

pinocchio
nation

embracing truth in a culture of lies

INCLUDES A PERSONAL INTEGRITY WORKBOOK

PIÑON PRESS

P.O. Box 35007, Colorado Springs, CO 80935

OUR GUARANTEE TO YOU

We believe so strongly in the message of our books that we are making this quality guarantee to you. If for any reason you are disappointed with the content of this book, return the title page to us with your name and address and we will refund to you the list price of the book. To help us serve you better, please briefly describe why you were disappointed. Mail your refund request to: PiñonPress, P.O. Box 35002, Colorado Springs, CO 80935.

Library of Congress Catalog Card Number: 00-065275
ISBN 1-57683-224-4

Cover illustration by Tony Stone Images/Peter Samuels
Cover design by Ray Moore
Design Team: Brad Lewis, Amy Spencer, Glynese Northam

Some of the anecdotal illustrations in this book are true to life and are included with the permission of the persons involved. All other illustrations are composites of real situations, and any resemblance to people living or dead is coincidental.

Scripture quotations in this publication are taken from the *Holy Bible: New International Version*® (NIV®). Copyright © 1973, 1978, 1984 by International Bible Society. Used by permission of Zondervan Publishing House. All rights reserved.

This publication is designed to provide accurate and authoritative information in regard to the subject matter covered. It is sold with the understanding that the author and the publisher are not engaged in rendering legal, accounting, or other professional service. If legal advice or other expert assistance is required, the services of a competent professional person should be sought. *From a Declaration of Principles jointly adopted by a Committee of the American Bar Association and a Committee of Publishers.*

Donaldson, Devlin, 1957-
  Pinocchio nation / Devlin Donaldson and Steve Wamburg.
    p. cm.
  "Includes a personal integrity workbook."
    ISBN 1-57683-224-4
    1. Truthfulness and falsehood--Religious aspects--Christianity.   I. Wamburg, Steve.
II. Title
BV4627.F3.D66 2001
241'.673--dc21   00-065274

Printed in the United States of America

1 2 3 4 5 6 7 8 9 10 / 04 03 02 01

pinocchio
nation

embracing truth in a culture of lies

To our fathers, Bob Donaldson and Don Wamberg,
good and decent men for whom truth was an everyday habit.
In spite of potential outcomes, they always shot straight with
everyone. Especially their own sons. Truth matters to us
because in no uncertain terms it did to them.

"Way down, in our heart of hearts,
we know we are fortunate men. . . . "

► Contents

► Acknowledgments

While it may only take weeks or months to actually write a book, the reality is that you have been preparing for a lifetime. It's impossible to thank everyone who has impacted your life. But every author has to try. So here are our lists of those who have helped prepare us.

Devlin:

I'd like to thank my family. First and foremost, thanks to my wife, Carol, and my daughter, Maria, for love, joy, patience, and so much more. Your sacrifices are huge and do not go unnoticed. Thanks to my mother and sister for raising me and growing up with me respectively.

To my coauthor Steve Wamberg: It was twenty-five years ago we hooked up on this journey. What a ride! We have a lot further to go. I can't wait.

There are those who have helped prepare me. To them I owe so much. Thanks to Dr. Gary Collins for believing in me and encouraging me to work at writing. I don't think we could have imagined twenty years ago what we would have been through together. To Stuart Ryder, who helped me learn how to think (what a gift!). Press Webster, you're gone but not forgotten. M. L. Hillard, one of the best teachers I have ever known. Dr. Robert Erickson and Dr. Richard Bescanson, thank you for helping to bring structure to the unruly mind of a young, wild student.

There are those who have talked with me about the material in this book, others who read early versions of chapters and offered their insights. Dr. Molly Davis Scott, thanks for your encouragement and support. Rev. Jimmy Sites, you are an inspiration and an encouragement far beyond what you might think. George Barna, thanks for being a friend and for so generously offering us the use of some of your valuable research as we worked on this book.

Barry Strickland, thanks for your role in helping me face the truth about myself. It has been life changing. Larry, for everything. And Tony, words aren't sufficient. You two are the brothers I never had. Thanks also to Joey and Mark Hanlon, Sam and T-Bone Burnett, and Bill and Nancy Tibert for real friendship.

And to the man who has represented me, Robert Wolgemuth, thanks for the years of working together. It has been wonderful. Piñon Press, thanks for seeing the need for this book and working with us.

Steve:

There's no way to be a happy writer without an exceptional family. I thank God for mine. Annie, your patience and love keep me sane when I don't deserve to be. Ben and Maggie, you both show me understanding beyond your years. I love you and I'm proud of your own successes in telling and hearing the truth.

Mom, watching you craft your columns let me know that this way of life wasn't the easiest, but hitting a nerve is worth the trouble. Thanks for all your love and advice. I listened even when I didn't follow it to the letter.

Pete and Susie, Jim and Kathy, Don and Pam, and Marty and Hank: Your ongoing willingness to keep the coffee warm and the porch lights burning over the years has made us friends as well as siblings. I owe you more than you'll ever know.

Devlin, we've discovered what our fathers told us is true. Time to make more of it, wouldn't you say? Thanks for the easiest book I've ever coauthored.

Mentors have changed my life. Steve Swanson made me believe I had something worth saying, and taught me how from junior high on. Maro Craig, my grandpa Roy Knopp, and my dad demonstrated just how much wisdom can come through a well-spun story. Clyde and Betty Harmon have always been ready to help me think and rethink truth, the gospel, and the culture. Reidar Bjornard, Tom Finger, and Ray Bakke all challenged me to engage my brain and write about things that matter. I hope this counts.

Doug Loomer, Steve Shafer, Jerald January, and Jared McCarthy: You told me so, and knew me better than I did. Dana and Pam, Kirk and Deb, Al and Marilyn, Michael Jones, Jim and Eta, Barb and Woody, James Skeet, Dan and Dina, John Conaway, Sue and Gary, Tommy Moore, Jim and Jean, Dave and Maryellen, Thelma, and Steve and Amanda, thanks for taking me to the wall time and again with issues and reality—and loving me in the process.

Tony and D'Reen, thank you for adopting us. That goes for our extended family at Highland Park, too.

Special thanks is due to Lee and Maureen Geary of Pike's Perk ("Coffee with an Altitude"), Garland and Bridget Johnson and the entire UKKSA family, George Barna, Robert Wolgemuth, and Jennifer Cortez. Also to Brad Lewis and the staff at Piñon Press for their profound patience and encouragement on many fronts.

▶ Introduction

The insincerity of man—all men are liars or partial hiders of facts, half tellers of truths, shirks, moral sneaks. When a merely honest man appears he is a comet—his fame eternal—needs no genius, no talent—mere honesty—Luther, Christ, etc.
—Mark Twain

When we can on Saturdays, we spend an hour or two over coffee. We cover a wide variety of subjects. We unload about work, our families, theology, politics, complexity theory, the arts, college football, and the state of the culture in general. Then we buy our second cup of coffee and begin again.

Not long ago, over biscotti on such a Saturday, Steve was wrapped up in making a point and began a statement with "Well, the truth be told . . . "

For some reason, at that moment, the phrase stopped Devlin dead in his tracks. He'd heard those words before. In fact, they had become a kind of stock phrase in our everyday conversations. But this time "the truth be told" took Devlin far away from the dialogue at hand and down another track: *So, what is Wamberg saying here? Why does he have to reassure me that he's telling me the truth? Isn't truth the basis of our relationship? Is what he's about to say so incredible that he needs to let me know that he understands the outrageous parameters of his statement?*

Meanwhile, Steve rambled on about the virtues of option football. (He's a Nebraska fan from way back.)

The flood of questions continued in Devlin's mind, and revealed a darker current: *Was he telling me the truth about other things he didn't qualify? Or were those statements at least not held to the same standard of truthfulness? Or was the statement he was making not true and he was setting me up by reassuring me of its veracity? Can I really count on anything my friend is saying?*

By this time it was evident that Devlin was no longer actively engaged in the conversation at hand. Steve stopped, leaned across the table, and caught Devlin's eye. "Dev, where are you?"

"Oh. Sorry. Just . . . well, you said 'the truth be told.'"

"I did? Okay, what about it?"

"I say it a lot these days. I wonder why."

"It's a phrase that allows you to gather your thoughts for the next sentence?"

"Sometimes. But where did it come from? Why did anyone ever feel a need to remind—no—warn someone else that they were telling the truth?"

That made the conversation shift gears.

We talked about our dads, and how truth was an expectation—no exceptions—growing up. We talked about Harry Truman and Mark Twain and how refreshing they were for their straightforwardness. We offered each other examples from business and personal lives where truth was rewarded, and where truth was ignored or even punished.

We talked about how we were raising our own children with an appreciation for the truth. As products of two fine seminaries, we talked about Christian ethics. As consultants, we talked about media and press "spin" and about where lines could be drawn between reality and fantasy in businesses and organizations. We talked about telling our wives the truth when it wasn't always comfortable. We told stories of our own failures with the truth, and of some successes.

And in the course of that conversation, we realized that telling and hearing the truth were no longer "givens" in our culture. We wondered what we'd look like as a "Pinocchio nation." How long would our noses be if they grew every time we dodged the truth?

At the very least, people wouldn't be turning their heads very quickly in a crowded bus.

But how did we get here as a society? What's so hard about the truth that we collectively avoid it rather than embrace it? In an age of "moral sneaks," we ask with Mark Twain, "Where are the 'merely honest' people?" And, "How do I become one?"

These questions brought to light a number of issues regarding truth and its practice that we felt we needed to explore. This book comes from our exploration. In the first section, we discuss the role and impact of truth in everyday life, along with a notion we call the "Rule of Truth," which calls for each of us to allow truth to be an equal-opportunity offender of ourselves as well as those around us. In the second section, we take a look at truth in spirituality, the family, the workplace, and society at large. In the final section, we examine what we're handing off to the next generation in regard to truth, and what we can do to practically enhance the place of truth in everyday life with "Fourteen Tactics for Telling the Truth." (There are actually exercises to do to help you put truth into practice.) Truth is an ideal, but it's an ideal that calls for practical application.

That's why we freely mixed the philosophical and the practical in the pages that follow. Strange as it may seem, what follows isn't too far removed from our Saturday afternoon discussions over coffee: eclectic, passionate, sometimes a little off-the-wall. We hope it gives you some fresh ideas about the place of truth in your own life.

It did for us.

Devlin Donaldson and Steve Wamberg
Colorado Springs, Colorado

section one

embracing truth in a culture of lies

the role of truth the role of

Chapter

1 ▶ the role of truth

Truthfulness is a condition of any collective undertaking.
—Ralph B. Perry

Have you heard the story of the farmer and the baker who had a bartering agreement? Every day, Zeke the farmer would exchange a pound of butter for Louie the baker's pound of bread. It wasn't long before Louie felt he was being cheated—and in fact, when Louie carefully checked the butter's weight, he found out he was being shortchanged.

He immediately took Zeke to court (this story obviously comes from a culture nearly as litigious as ours). Louie was angry as he laid his argument out before the magistrate. "I know I'm not getting a pound of butter for the bread I give to Zeke!" he said heatedly.

The magistrate, hoping to bring both parties to a peaceful settlement, asked Zeke, "Sir, let's start by checking the weights you use to measure the pound of butter you give to your friend, the baker."

Zeke responded, "Don't have any weights, your honor."

Louie smiled to himself. This case was about to settle in his favor. What was this hayseed thinking, anyway, trying to do business without weights?

The magistrate continued. "Then how do you measure the butter?"

Zeke shrugged. "Well, your honor, I just use the weight of the one-pound loaf he gives me to measure the weight of the butter. Seems to me that if he's short on the butter, then I'm short on the bread."

Case dismissed.

Discussions of truth are long and esoteric. This one isn't. We can't afford to complicate the argument here because we have a more practical aim with this book. We're here to remind ourselves that truth—real, everyday truth—is at issue in every day, in every relationship. Compromising the truth is serious business, and we can do that at any moment. But at what cost? That's a crucial question if you believe, as we do, that "truthfulness is a condition of any collective undertaking."

If truth doesn't have that role, we're all at risk. Who is cheated when truth isn't given its proper role in our everyday social contracts? Who loses when truth isn't valued, much less put into practice? The ultimate answer: Everyone. When one side is "short on the butter," the other side is "short on the bread." That means trust is violated, and that negates the role of truth in our collective undertakings: to build trust.

The Magistrate's Question: What's Your Standard?

Let's go back to the magistrate's question. We need to examine our standard. We need to know what we're using as weights.

What's your standard definition for truth? For starters, we could just look at what the dictionary says. *Webster's New World Dictionary (Second College Edition)* says some of the following things when defining truth: "the quality or state of being true, the quality of being in accordance with experience, facts or reality; conformity with fact, agreement with a standard rule, etc.; that accords with fact or reality."

There's a wonderful Greek word, *alatheia,* which means "truth." One day in Greek class (many years ago) we ventured to ask, "So how would ancient Greeks have defined 'truth'?"

The wise professor responded, "It would have been a little more visceral than *Webster's.* Something like 'the stuff reality is made of.'" Huh? "The stuff . . . reality . . . is made of." Okay.

Of course, these definitions assume that we're able to sort out facts and tell them truthfully.

If truth is the stuff reality is made of, that means it has little to do with long philosophical arguments. Instead, truth is how you answer your children's questions. It's how you address your boss's concerns. It's how you act out your responsibility to your community.

Whose Reality: The Peril of Postmodern Truth

Lyricist Time Rice caught the conscience of a generation in the rock opera *Jesus Christ Superstar* when he recounted (and expanded on) the exchange between Jesus and Pontius Pilate as found in the gospel of John in the Bible. The discussion focused on the question, "What is truth?"

Pilate did his level best in the dialogue to suggest that *his* standard of truth was different from Jesus'. Therefore, as his thinking went, Pilate would not have to deal with the possibilities of truth Jesus presented. Pilate could, in good conscience, ignore the possibility that Jesus' understanding of truth was relevant to his Roman outlook.

Rice's rendition is a model of the ongoing ambivalence about truth that marks the postmodern society we find ourselves in. While there's no singular view as to what postmodernism is, the commonly held postmodern approach to applying truth in everyday life stems from this premise: Everyone has her own experience and own truth. That premise produces these results:

▶ Whatever is right for you is right for you and is beyond questioning by anyone else.

▶ I can believe whatever I want, no matter how inherently contradictory or logically flawed my belief is.

▶ You have the right to define truth any way you feel is appropriate—as long as you aren't imposing your view on others.

What postmodern thought boils down to is *relativism.* So what's the problem with relativism? In his book *True for You, but Not for Me,* Paul Copan directly addresses this question.

The claims of relativists are like saying "I can't speak a word of English" or "All generalizations are false." Our most basic reply to the relativist is that his statements are self-contradictory. They self-destruct. They are self-undermining. The relativist actually falsifies his own system by his self-referential statements like everyone's beliefs are true or false only relative to himself. If the claims are only true to the speaker, then his claims are only true to himself. It is difficult to see why his claims should matter to us.[1]

Zeke the farmer and Louie the baker each had his own "standard" for truth. Instead of measuring honestly against a common standard of reality, each created his own standard for his own benefit.

The adoption of individual standards against everyday reality is the paradox of postmodern thought. It's something each of us faces every day: whose truth is it, anyway?

Take the teenager (okay, it was Steve) who found himself out past curfew one Saturday night. Steve realized that this crisp autumn evening was the night the clocks "fell back" from Daylight Savings Time to Standard Time. If he made it home within an hour of curfew, he'd still be safe.

Breakfast conversation the next morning went like this: Steve's dad began with the obvious question, "What time did you get home last night?"

Steve responded, "Well, Dad, that depends on which time we were negotiating with when I went out. I was home on time according to this morning's clock."

From this point, the argument for "relative standards" went out the window. Steve's father made it clear that the clock as it was Saturday night when Steve left was the stuff that curfew reality was made of!

From curfews to contracts, truth has a starting point. It begins in the facts of everyday life.

The Importance of Truth — and Believability

Before we go much further, it's important that we begin to clearly define some terms. We'll talk about "telling the truth" in this book. *That means that when we speak, we're doing our best to line up what we say with the facts as we know them.*

Edward R. Murrow, the icon of twentieth-century journalism, thought truth was important in his day—and on the job. That's why he developed this credo for journalists:

- ▶ To be persuasive, we must be believable,
- ▶ To be believable, we must be credible,
- ▶ To be credible, we must be truthful.[2]

The role of truth still seems to be important. "Living with a high degree of integrity" was listed as a top priority for nearly 87 percent of respondents in the United States in a recent Barna Research Group survey.[3]

That makes sense. Truth—alignment with facts, dealing with the stuff of reality—makes or breaks our everyday credibility. We want to fulfill our social contracts, and to be able to trust others in those contracts. Still, we must have some consensus for the standards of truth, or we won't believe each other.

When you study geometry, you systematically learn certain axioms that allow you to create theorems. You can prove the theorems with axioms, but axioms are simply givens. You can use both to solve problems.

Every society assumes certain values (axioms). They're assumed because they're the building blocks used to make the machinery of living work. They're foundational beliefs that allow us to approach and ultimately solve our problems.

But what are our axioms today? Do we have agreement, or does the standard for truth fluctuate between us? Another Barna Research Group survey asked respondents if they agreed with the following statement: "There is no such thing as absolute truth; two people could define truth in totally conflicting ways but both could still be correct." More than 30 percent of those surveyed agreed strongly; nearly 40 percent agreed somewhat; 10 percent disagreed somewhat; and 15 percent disagreed strongly.[4] So even if we claim that the role of truth is important, the majority of us believe that the standards and definitions of truth are flexible.

Where does that leave us? Clearly, when we begin to bend the standards, we warp the truth. When facts are negotiable, truth is a commodity with uncertain value. That creates uncertainty rather than trust in our "collective undertakings" at home, church, work—even when we look at ourselves in the mirror.

Whose truth do you use? Because we mentioned the mirror, let's take an everyday example from our national infatuation with it: Are you overweight? "Well, if you use those insurance charts, yes," you say. "Thirty pounds over on the chart. But isn't everyone overweight on these things except those 'starving model' types? Hey, and there's my nephew who weighs more than I do, and he's an inch shorter than I am."

"Yeah, according to the insurance charts, of course I'm overweight," says your nephew the weightlifter. "But I only carry 2.8 percent body fat. So that standard doesn't apply to me."

"Hmmm. So if I lifted weights, I could weigh this much and still not be overweight," you think.

"Here, have another piece of pie." It's Mom. You always look malnourished to Mom, even with your belly hanging two inches past your cinched belt. Overweight? Not in her universe. Good old Mom . . .

Whose standard? Whose truth? What is the stuff that makes up reality? Well, Mom is biased. She might not be the one you should ask about your appearance. Your nephew has no neck and his biceps are roughly the size of your thighs. Are you really going to lift weights, anyway? The standard of reality says you may need a close look at the chart and a talk with your doctor. Then you'd better be ready to respond to the truth about your weight.

We believe that telling the truth is one of those basic human values that is necessary to make things work. Assuming we share the same standards for truth—not a good assumption today—the task of being able to face the truth about ourselves is where things must start. Then telling those in your family the truth, both about themselves and about yourself, is foundational to relationship. And relationship is built on trust.

Truth and Trust

In her autobiography, *Somebody to Love,* Grace Slick, former lead singer of the '60s San Francisco band Jefferson Airplane, talks briefly about truth: "The French have a phrase, *petit mort,* which means 'little death.' . . . When people lie to you, it's a little death—the death of trust."[5]

Clearly, the concept of truth isn't something limited to conservatives, those without some sense of adventure, or those who simply hold to a strong Judeo-Christian ethic. Even an avant-garde rock-and-roller understands that relationship is based on trust.

And trust is virtually impossible without truthfulness.

To tell the truth (oops), most of us don't tell the truth under some illusion that we're saving the person we lie to (there, we said it: "we lie") from some sort of pain. In reality, our practice of lying in social contracts only sets others up for even more pain.

Sometimes this sort of lying happens in the workplace. Bill was a friend of ours who wasn't quite meeting standards where he worked. For whatever reason, no one told Bill the truth about his performance during reviews. Bill continued working every day under the impression that things were fine on the job. But as time went on, his lack of performance became more obvious. In the company's eyes, quick action had to be taken—and no wonder. Bill walked in one morning to find an invitation to visit the human resources department, which promptly escorted him from the building permanently.

"Good old Bill" wasn't helped by his supervisor's desire to protect his feelings. And if Bill were a vindictive soul, he might have been able to build a case for constructive termination against his former employer.

So just who do we protect when we deny the truth? You might be able to make a case for protecting those that we supposedly care about (although we'll address that later). The obvious answer is that we're clearly saving *ourselves* from the pain of disclosure—whether disclosure of self, of unfortunate facts, or of revelatory insights.

Truth is important as a concept, but it's also at least as important as a *behavior*. That means we have to *tell* the truth as well as believe it. We need to treat the truth not simply as something we practice. Truth-telling allows us to build relationships with ourselves, our family, those we work with, and society at large. While we can all say that we believe in telling the truth, the influence of "situation ethics" or "values clarification" seems to have eroded our character. We've been seduced into a false understanding of the role of truth.

Situation ethics and values clarification seem to share the philosophy that says lying is ethically sound as long as it is done for a higher good. In fairness, truth is a value to the situation ethicist, but not a high enough one to take precedence over other factors.

An example: Was it all right for citizens who hid Jews from the Nazis to lie about the whereabouts of the Jews they were hiding? The situation ethicist would build an argument that says the situation overrides the value of truth; therefore, lying was alright in that situation.

The situation ethicists aren't alone. Some other philosophers and theologians have constructed arguments to give people moral permission to avoid truth altogether. They also offer cases like the one mentioned above to prove their point. Would we allow them these extreme exceptions put into practice? Probably, as long as we all remembered that such cases are exceptions.

Why? Because such incidents are so highly isolated that they should have little if any impact on everyday behavior. Unfortunately, what has happened in the wake of our culture's philosophy is the deconstruction of truth as a value. We've steadily and mistakenly applied this "ethics of the exception" to the ethics of the everyday. We've mutated the cultural role of truth from that of building trust—even of regarding its role for higher purposes—into that of justifying our own ends, regardless of others' well-being.

The recent legal maneuvers that had the president of the United States asking his court questioners to define the meaning of the word "is" is an outrageous exercise in mincing and hairsplitting words. It's also simply a reflection of Zeke the farmer's attitude: "Don't have any weights, so I'll just use the weights you give me." (Or "I'll define what 'weights' are.")

How painfully short the journey is from torturing language to the compromise of any standard for truth-telling. How quickly we stumble to the edge of this cliff: "I don't have any standards for truth, so I'll take yours. If they don't suit my goals in this exchange, I'll define my own."

Truth-telling, to ourselves or to those around us, doesn't guarantee a happy ending. It doesn't ensure that things will work out the way we intended them to. But what truth-telling does is ensure a clean process that works itself through in our lives. It allows us to live our lives with dignity, integrity, and a decided lack of fear. Tell the truth: you won't fear being found out. Tell the truth: you won't fear someone discovering your secret and revealing it to those from whom you've hidden it.

Ethicist Sissela Bok lays out this simple connection between truth and trust:

> I can have different types of trust: that you will treat me fairly, that you will have my interests at heart, that you will do me no harm. But if I do not trust your word, can I have genuine trust in the first three? If there is no confidence in the truthfulness of others, is there any way to assess their fairness, their intentions to help or to harm? How, then, can they be trusted? Whatever matters to human beings, trust is the atmosphere in which it thrives.[6]

Both of us enjoy truth-based relationships with our wives. Sure, we disagree about many things. The disagreements are exciting (in their own ways) and may often be followed by fireworks. But we're both confident that, no matter how painful it is to hear our wives' versions of the truth, we can trust them to tell us the impact of facts—from an unfulfilled promise to one of our children to the fact that we'll likely never fit into those jeans we wore in grad school—upon them.

In any such encounter, one of the partner's interpretations of the facts is bound to be incorrect, skewed, or misinterpreted. (Both of us openly admit that our wives seem to be growing more astute as time passes.) But we know our wives are being truthful with us about how those facts have affected them in the relevant area of their lives: emotionally, spiritually, and/or physically.

Partners in marriage need to offer each other the truth. When the truth is mutually exercised in marriage, a couple can do the homework it takes to work through the difficulties any relationship encounters. In our own marriages, telling the truth has been a "character builder." How character matures, grows, and becomes strong in a marriage is often measured by our ability to tell the truth in the context of a loving covenant.

Strong, resilient character can bear the pain of telling the truth. It can carry the weight of hearing the truth. The more we deal in the truth, the more familiar we are with it. We can be hurt less by the truth if we've accepted certain things as being truth.

We can trust the truth to build a relationship if our intent is to do so. We can also expect a lie to break down a relationship.

That Knot in Your Stomach

We both enjoyed rather idyllic childhoods. At least, that's how we remember them.

Remember those summers when you were old enough to do some things on your own but still too young for a summer job? Devlin spent those summers of his late elementary years with a special group of neighborhood friends. During school months they were still a group, but those glorious summer months gave them the opportunity to really talk about life. They would all talk about the things in their lives that mattered, most of which they knew little about. As part of the process, they'd try to "outdo" each other. Someone's story would set off a response of "Oh, get outta here! That's a lie if I ever heard one!" Instead of admitting to an overstatement or outright fantasy, though, the "storyteller" would concoct tales that would somehow support the story told. Of course, these bordered on the fantastic, too. All this effort in building a parallel universe was spent to avoid conflict, to remain a part of the group.

Devlin remembers more than a few long, hot summer evenings when he'd lie awake in bed, worried that he'd tripped up. He'd go over the events and conversations of the day to see if he'd opened himself up to more conflict the next day based on his lies that day.

Admit it: You've had nights like that, too. You've felt the same knot thicken in your stomach. At one time or another you've prayed for the ability to keep all the different strands of your stories unraveling in such a way that they would never touch.

At about the same time Devlin was having stomach knots over stories in Ohio, Steve was figuring out cover stories for late-night escapades in southwest Iowa.

We've all had nights like that, with those panicked moments when we might have jeopardized something by lying. The fact is, unless we learned the lesson as a youngster, we live with the same knot all these years later.

It just gets thicker.

Hiding from the Truth

We can enjoy a multitude of benefits from embracing the truth. But our natural human response seems to be to run from it.

Remember the story of Adam and Eve? After doing the one thing God told them not to do, Adam and Eve hid themselves. When finally confronted with the truth of their actions, they did what every single one of us did at some time when we were children and were caught doing something we knew we shouldn't do.

They lied. But why?

We believe that people fear the truth for a number of reasons. The fear of consequence is one of those reasons. Or perhaps we fear reprisal. In other instances, we fear being faced with something about ourselves that we can't, won't, or don't want to change. Sometimes we fear conflict. We also fear being shamed.

Isn't it strange that denying the truth puts us in a posture of fear? And, that being said, is it any less mature for a child to be afraid of the dark than it is for an adult to be afraid of the light?

For years, Marge held a horrible secret from her husband, Sid: She had been sexually abused by her stepbrother over a five-year period in late childhood. This was no "dredge up the hidden memories" experience. It was real. She'd even reported the ongoing reality to her mother and stepfather throughout that time. They just denied that it was happening. They never confronted Marge's stepbrother. The abuse ended only when he moved out of the house.

It wasn't long into their marriage that Sid began to question her about their lack of intimacy. "Honey, is it something I've said? Something I've done?"

Marge's lack of disclosure allowed Sid's imagination to run wild. Finally, he lost confidence in his ability to be a husband. He quit initiating romantic interludes. He stopped talking with Marge when he came home from work.

Marge might have lived with that secret all through her life. But she loved Sid too much to let him fall apart. She did the loving and difficult thing to do: she told her story to Sid. The pain of the encounters, the insecurity of not knowing if or when the next one could happen, the hurt of her parents' denial—it all came pouring out.

And Sid understood. The truth healed them both. This wasn't a fairytale ending—they still had to go through counseling. But the light of the truth took the relationship out of the dark.

Okay, So Why Truth, Again?

Truth is important because as humans we live in relationships. Its role is to build trust in every dimension of our relationships. We believe that people live in relationship with God, with other individuals, and also with themselves. Truth-telling is crucial in each aspect of relationship—starting with ourselves.

If we lie to ourselves, we can never improve, build on our strengths, or buttress our weaknesses. We hinder our own development. As a consequence, we may never build the character it takes to trust even ourselves.

If we lie to others, we deny them the basis for building relationships with us. We sacrifice the common good for personal advantage. As a consequence, the fabric of human society—held together by the delicate threads of relationships—is weakened.

And if we lie to God, we show the cycle of self-deception to be complete. Who are we kidding at that point, anyway? As a consequence, we become more inclined to place ourselves at the center of the universe and to "play God" with ever-decreasing regard for the quality of our relationships.

We all deal with the stuff that reality is made of. We all have an inherent responsibility to give truth its proper role in everyday life. We all have some means to come to a common agreement about standards of reality so we can exercise meaningful exchange surrounding events and their impact.

The role of truth is to build trust. We must take every possible opportunity to give truth its proper role in everyday life. We must become everyday truth-tellers. Otherwise, we'll all be short on the "bread and butter" of a healthy life: sound relationships.

the rule of truth the rule of truth the rule of truth the
rule of truth the rule of truth the rule of truth the rule
of truth the rule of truth the rule of truth the rule of
truth the rule of truth the rule of truth the rule
of truth the rule of truth the rule of truth the rule of
truth the rule of truth the rule of truth the rule
of truth the rule of truth the rule of truth the rule of

Chapter

2 ▶ the rule of truth

If you do not tell the truth about yourself you cannot tell it about other people.
—Virginia Woolf

Mel thoroughly enjoyed his friend Ralph, even though it seemed they were pre-destined to take the opposite ends of any discussion even before it started.

This particular day was no exception. Mel had fired the opening salvo over their weekly Tuesday lunch appointment. "Ralph, I think truth is a victim of our age. Very few people care about it. Advertisers and preachers stretch it, the media abuse it, and . . . "

Ralph washed down a mouthful of salad while he waved his hand to inter-rupt. "Excuse me, Mel. There's a reason for that. Nobody we know likes the truth—especially the truth about themselves."

"But how do we have any kind of relationship without the truth? Complete honesty has to be the basis of any human contract worth pursuing."

"Yeah, sure. Right. Truth is a virtue. But does that mean anything anymore?"

"It does to me." The second the words escaped his lips, Mel knew Ralph was about to close in for the kill.

"Wait a minute—is it just me, or is that your own nose growing there, Pinocchio?"

"Whaddya mean by that?"

"No offense intended. Truth works as a virtue because *that* doesn't take any application in the real world. Enjoy your belief system, buddy. Just don't try to make it into too much more."

"But it is more than that! It's . . . it's the right thing."

"Naïve, simplistic, and reactionary."

"And you've never really addressed truth as the basis for a relationship."

Ralph snorted with pleasure. It was obvious that he felt he had Mel backed into a conversational corner. "Child's play. Start with your lovely bride, Naomi." Ralph's eyebrows formed an arch parallel to his smirk as he leaned over to whisper conspiratorially, "What if Naomi asks you how she looks—and she looks terrible?"

And with that, Ralph leaned back to stab the Tuesday salmon special before him, relishing the moment as he awaited Mel's reply.

The unspoken accusation in Ralph's question was clear: *The truth means nothing here, even to you. Of course, you won't tell your wife that she looks horrible. You'll lie to her and tell her that she looks beautiful, right?*

Well, maybe—but maybe not in the way you're thinking.

Liar, Liar

This theme was explored in the recent film *Liar, Liar*. Jim Carrey's character, Fletcher Reede, uses this example to explain to his son, Max, why adults need to lie:

> When your mommy was pregnant with you she gained a good forty pounds. There was nothing that she wouldn't eat—and Daddy was scared. But when she would ask me, "Honey, how do I look?" I'd say, "Honey, you look great. You're beautiful. You're glowing." If I had told Mommy she looked like a cow, it would have hurt her feelings. Do you understand?[1]

Who can't relate to this example? How do you apply the truth in this situation? Amazingly, the movie also provides a classic answer. Max's simple reply to his father's huge rationalization is this: "My teacher says real beauty is on the inside."

In this simple illustration, we begin to see how we as individuals—and as communities and society—rationalize a lie. Truth is an equal opportunity offender. It deserves a just application to everyone. And we believe that application begins *for* each one of us *in* each one of us.

That being said, truth has a bad reputation these days. Former statesman Adlai Stevenson had it right when he said, "You will find that the truth is often unpopular. . . . For, in the vernacular, we Americans are suckers for good news."[2] According to a recent Barna Research Group survey, nearly one-third of us believe to some degree that "the way things are today, lying is sometimes necessary."[3]

Suckers for good news, indeed. We've become so lazy in our approach to life that we quickly and simply go for the easiest way out of any situation. Sadly, "necessary lying" usually starts with the person we see in the mirror. We want the truth applied to anyone *but* ourselves. As a result, we can diffuse our responsibility to tell the truth in several ways.

Using Truth as a Shield

Many people use the "truth" as a shield. In fact, probably all of us do it at some time. Using the truth as a shield means simply taking a position that has at least some elements of the truth embedded in it. Then we use those elements of truth to inoculate ourselves against having someone tell us an unpleasant truth about ourselves or our situation.

Here's a classic and tragic example from modern marriage. (We'll be talking more about truth-telling in the family context in a later chapter, too.) We will use a hypothetical couple, Malcolm and Jonna, to illustrate "truth abuse" in a relationship. (What we are about to unpack, however, are all actual instances from marriages we've known.)

Here's the "truth abuse" from Jonna, who had married Malcolm right out of college: "I don't know why we're getting a divorce. I guess we just fell out of love."

This came after nearly twenty years together and raising two children. "Just falling out of love" seemed a bit weak, but it did have some elements of truth in it. Jonna and Malcolm were no longer blissfully married. In fact, it seemed as though they were both doing their best to make each other miserable.

The truth began to show itself as the weeks passed. Jonna and Malcolm had nurtured a friendship with another couple from Jonna's workplace. Jonna and the husband of the other couple shared time together at work as well. When pressed for the truth, Jonna admitted that they had openly talked about leaving their spouses for each other. Jonna was not at all comfortable pursuing those thoughts while she was still married to Malcolm, so she began distancing herself from her husband. Malcolm responded by distancing himself, and flirting openly with other women.

Jonna was about to get her wish of freedom through divorce. Through her actions, she'd also managed to convince Malcolm that someone else was better suited to be his wife. (Great basis for a healthy marriage, don't you think?)

"Falling out of love" didn't just happen. It began as a conscious choice of both Jonna and Malcolm. Jonna had accurately described her present feeling, but had failed to engage the more complete truth about her choices that helped her feel that way.

It's the pattern here that illustrates using truth as a shield. Instead of confessing to the act, acknowledging the decisions that led to the situation, or in some other way owning up to the real situation, the person grabs a little truth and confesses to "following my heart instead of my mind." As true as that may be, it's still a rationalization that allows the person to opt out of any real responsibility for his actions.

Truth as a Weapon

One of the most common misuses of the truth is when it is used as a weapon against others.

Let's continue with the story of Malcolm and Jonna. When Jonna first began distancing herself from Malcolm, he was deeply hurt. He tried the flowers-and-once-a-week-to-dinner approach to spark the relationship. When Jonna didn't respond as Malcolm expected, the hurt became anger.

He decided to recite a litany of the things that had bothered him about Jonna since the day they'd met as freshmen in college. Each item on his list was factual. The list covered Jonna's preference for romantic comedies and her refusal over the years to sit and watch even one football game with him. Malcolm's list also noted Jonna's inability to balance the household checkbook even though she was trained in accounting, and that he always came off as the hard guy in disciplining the children. In fact, he even managed to dredge up the fact that she lined up her French fries on her plate according to size when she was in high school. (He remembered a conversation with one of Jonna's friends at a class reunion to come up with that little tidbit.)

Need we say that was a bad move on Malcolm's part? In this case and any other like it, using the truth as a weapon *isn't* about telling the truth. It's about exacting a pound of flesh. It's a tool to achieve revenge, pure and simple. The very intent of revenge, even though the words you say may be reflecting the truth, makes this tactic less about truth and more about inflicting pain.

Truth as Diversion

In heated situations, comments can get a little too personal. Things can be said that are hurtful, vindictive, or maybe just a little too close to the truth for our own comfort. One unfortunate response in those situations is to employ the tactic of using truth as a diversion. When we simply are unwilling, unready, or incapable of hearing the truth about ourselves, we use some "truth arrows" of our own to shoot out the lights that are being turned toward us.

Let's continue with the "truth abuses" of Malcolm and Jonna. Jonna, in response to Malcolm's attacks with truth, responded with, "Well, you haven't watched your weight since we left college. It surprises me that any of the women you talk to can give you a second look, except out of pity."

Ouch! Like many of us, Malcolm indeed lost his svelte figure by the age of thirty—and it bothered him to no end. Jonna knew that, so she told a truth about Malcolm where he was quite vulnerable. This dislodged Malcolm's confidence and sent him down a mental track that made him wonder if his marriage would be as miserable had he stayed on a perpetual diet.

When we use truth as a diversion, we quickly try to remember some unsavory fact or insight into the person we're having the heated exchange with. We launch it like a missile into the conversation, hoping to inflict enough pain to end the discussion (at best) or at least to get the light turned around to make *the other person* the subject of the investigative discussion.

Truth as a shield, truth as a weapon, truth as a diversion—they're all examples of truth abuse. So how do we guard ourselves from such abuse? What could provide a practical standard for using truth well in every instance? Can we suggest the Rule of Truth?

Of course we can.

The Rule of Law

The political and legal discussions surrounding the 1998 impeachment hearings of President Clinton brought a concept called "the Rule of Law" into the public forum. This is a concept that the framers of the Constitution articulated, wrestled with, and ultimately incorporated into their thinking.

Simply put, the Rule of Law says that everyone must live under the law of the country. No one is excluded, immune, or exempt from the law. Whether or not someone has done something wrong is not based upon an opinion; it's based on the written law. The judgment of right and wrong is moved from the emotional arena and into an arena that is as objective as possible.

The Rule of Law provides equal protection for all citizens. It prevents ordinary citizens from receiving a brand of justice different from that received by an upper or ruling class. It is meant to be one of the great equalizers of our society. We may all choose to live our lives differently, we may all prosper differently, and we may all worship differently. But when it comes to our contract with society to live in a certain way, we're all held to the same standard. This Rule of Law, this equality of justice, is one of the unifying concepts of our society, one of the values that holds us together.

We believe there's a sound application of the Rule-of-Law logic to telling the truth. We call it "the Rule of Truth."

The Rule of Truth

The Rule of Truth, simply stated, is this:

> No one has the right to tell someone else "the truth" until they have spent the time, energy, and focus to learn the truth about themselves.

Sounds like a simple concept. It is, but the *application* of the Rule of Truth is anything but simple. The Rule of Truth requires an evenhanded application of the truth to yourself. That means you strive to honestly assess your liabilities and strengths, and then to act realistically in response to them.

Let's use an old Jewish folk tale to explain this. The story is told of a rabbi and three students who were walking between two towns one day. The rabbi wanted to test the students' abilities to candidly assess themselves. He asked them this question: "Suppose as we were traveling along this road we came across a bag full of gold. What would you do?"

One student answered without hesitation, "I'd return it to its owner." The rabbi stroked his beard and thought, *There's work left to do with this one. His answer came too quickly for him to have really considered the temptation.*

We agree: This student probably failed to rigorously apply the Rule of Truth to his own weaknesses.

The second student responded, "I would certainly fail here. If no one saw me, I'd keep the money." The rabbi raised one eyebrow in mild surprise and thought, *This one may know what tempts him, but where is his character? Would he succumb to temptation so easily?*

Again we agree: This student wasn't applying the Rule of Truth to himself, and so failed to recognize his reserves of strength.

The third student seemed reluctant to respond. After a few minutes, he raised his eyes to meet the rabbi's gaze and said, "Teacher, I know I would be tempted to take the bag for myself. So I would pray and ask God for the strength I would need to do what was right." The rabbi smiled and thought, *Finally! One of them has learned something.*

Indeed. The third student applied the Rule of Truth to himself with discipline. He didn't overestimate his assets, nor did he forget them. That allowed him to form a response to a situation, a response based on reality.

It wasn't easy. It took some thought. The payoff, though, is that the third student was prepared to deal with the stuff reality is made of.

The Source of the Rule of Truth

But where, you might ask, does this Rule of Truth come from? It comes from many places, but probably the most significant source this moral teaching stems from is the Bible.

There have been innumerable books about what the Bible has to say about truth, how it defines truth, and the moral laws that grow up around truth. It would be repetitive to attempt to cover all that ground again. But please allow us to note one biblical passage that the Rule of Truth is developed from:

> At dawn [Jesus] appeared again in the temple courts, where all the people gathered around him, and he sat down to teach them. The teachers of the law and the Pharisees brought in a woman caught in adultery. They made her stand before the group and said to Jesus, "Teacher, this woman was caught in the act of adultery. In the Law Moses commanded us to stone such women. Now what do you say?" They were using this question as a trap, in order to have a basis for accusing him.

But Jesus bent down and started to write on the ground with his finger. When they kept on questioning him, he straightened up and said to them, "If any one of you is without sin, let him be the first to throw a stone at her." Again he stooped down and wrote on the ground.

At this, those who heard began to go away one at a time, the older ones first, until only Jesus was left, with the woman still standing there. Jesus straightened up and asked her, "Woman, where are they? Has no one condemned you?"

"No one, sir," she said.

"Then neither do I condemn you," Jesus declared. "Go now and leave your life of sin." (John 8:2-11)

There's a lot going on in this story. The setting was a public place, the temple courts, where Jesus was teaching. The context lets us know that the debate regarding just who Jesus was occurred then in Israel much as it does in our culture today. He'd infuriated many of the religious leaders of his time. Little wonder, then, that the religious leaders in this passage were looking for a way to put Jesus in some kind of situation that could effectively end his ministry.

Their tactic was to use truth as a weapon. When they came to Jesus, they came prepared to make their point. They brought a woman to him who had been caught in adultery. Jewish law was unequivocal about this situation — she was to be stoned. But they made it a point to ask, "What do *you* say about stoning her according to the Law of Moses?"

With that question, they presented a profound dilemma to Jesus: If he agreed that the woman should be put to death, he'd put himself into direct conflict with the Roman government occupying Palestine at that time. Rome had decreed that Jews had no right to put anyone to death. But if Jesus excused the woman, the religious leaders could say that he was teaching others to ignore the Law of Moses.

They thought they had Jesus in an inescapable double bind. You can almost imagine them drooling as they waited to pounce on Jesus' answer.

Of course, they were expecting a more typical response than the one Jesus offered. When the case was posed to Jesus, he bent over and began to write in the dirt. There has been much speculation about what he was writing. Was he writing out what the Law said? Was he doodling in the dirt as he pondered what his response would be? Or maybe he was writing down some kind of accusation about others who were present. We simply can't say exactly what he was writing.

When Jesus stood up, he changed the question completely. It was no longer a question about what the Law said. *It was a question about how we use truth about others in relation to what we know about ourselves.* The woman was clearly guilty. But for Jesus, the question was no longer about what the Law said regarding her, but what the truth was about each one of those present. He challenged every person within hearing range to apply the Rule of Truth. Jesus put it this way: "If any one of you is without sin, let him be the first to throw a stone."

Jesus responded to the "truth abuse" in this situation. As we said earlier, truth was being used as a weapon in this case. It was meant to pierce Jesus and his work. Its intent was to ruin him somehow—if not at the hands of the religious leaders, then certainly at the hands of the Romans. It was never meant to help the accused woman. Those who were trying to trap Jesus had already reached their conclusions about her guilt and her penalty.

When Jesus spoke, he offered perhaps the clearest example of the principle we're calling the Rule of Truth. All those present were convicted, not by Jesus, not by the Pharisees, but by their own consciences. When those surrounding Jesus faced the truth about themselves, they were no longer able to be a part of a situation where truth was being used as a weapon. Truth could no longer be a means of vengeance.

Understand, the Rule of Truth is not meant to imply that we endorse any kind of behavior simply because we can be accused of something of equal gravity (or of a higher embarrassment quotient). The point of the Rule of Truth is that we handle truth in all situations quite differently once we have looked circumspectly at ourselves and faced our own shortcomings.

Probably the most important thing about truth is that we seek it. But a very close second is that we handle it well once we have it.

We're about to launch into an overview of the many ways the truth is abused, and of what can be done about it every day. But before we begin to speak out and try to advance the cause of truth at home, with our friends, at work, and in society, we have some preliminary work to do.

With the concept of the Rule of Truth established, we're going to look at what it means to look truthfully, honestly, and critically at ourselves. We'll explore our lives, what we might expect to find by applying the Rule of Truth, and how we should respond to the things we discover.

This process of self-discovery—"self-revelation" if you will—is not a one-time event. For the truth-teller, the application of the Rule of Truth will become a lifelong way of living. It's something we will use again and again. So let's look closely and find out some truth about ourselves as we begin this journey.

the impact of truth the impact of truth the impact
of truth the impact of truth the impact of truth the
impact of truth the impact of truth the impact of
truth the impact of truth the impact of truth the
impact of truth the impact of truth the impact of
truth the impact of truth the impact of truth the
impact of truth the impact of truth the impact of

Chapter

3 ▶ the impact of truth

Truth is a pain which will not stop.
—Louis-Ferdinand Céline

Hilda had been friends with Marian for the first forty-five years of their lives. They were school chums. They'd been in each other's wedding parties. They even married brothers, so they were related to each other to boot.

That's what made their falling out over the color scheme used in their church's nursery all the more tragic. Who knew that a lively discussion over whether to use primary colors or pastels for the "diaper brigade" would fuel a decades-long feud?

Thirty years after the rift began, Hilda went into the hospital for cancer surgery. Due to her age and the nature of the disease, her prognosis was gloomy. The women's husbands finally decided enough was enough. They demanded that the women reconcile before Hilda's surgery.

Marian was easy to convince. She felt no small amount of sorrow over her old friend's plight, and even some guilt for having wasted so many years in bitterness.

Hilda seemed less inclined to make the effort. Understandably, she was distracted by her own circumstances. Yet she saw the wisdom in making things right for the sake of their families.

Hilda and Marian had seemed to barely tolerate each other through years of family and church events. They'd been civil when they needed to be, but nothing more. A handshake in Hilda's hospital room seemed to be a bit formal for the situation, so they settled into a brief, stiff hug. Then they sat down, knee to knee, while their husbands stood at the doorway of the room.

Marian began. "Hilda, can you remember what drove us to this point?"

Hilda nodded. "The colors in the nursery." Then she visibly softened. "Do you know how many times they've repainted that room since then?"

Marian nodded her head. "It seems to be different every year or two. There's some kind of mural there now, isn't there?"

"It's been silly to keep up a fight over something that didn't last much past the day it was painted. What made us do that?"

"I don't know. I think I was afraid of you coming to me first and asking me to forgive you, and then I'd look ridiculous for making something so trivial into something so big."

"Honestly? I felt the same way. I was so scared all that time that you'd come along and want to reconcile, and then I'd look like a fool for getting into the argument in the first place."

The husbands looked at each other. It was about to happen. They were about to see success for their efforts.

The women said together, "Will you forgive me?" The expected tears and hugs followed. Then they spent the next few minutes trying to make up for thirty years of lost communication.

Marian knew Hilda needed to be well rested for the surgery, so she excused herself. Hilda watched her old friend go toward the door. Marian turned.

With a serious look on her face, Marian asked, "This still counts if you get better, doesn't it?"

Facing Pain

A surprising question? Not really. In fact, what kept both women from reconciling sooner was the pain of facing the truth about themselves. Marian just wanted to be sure that these recent reconciling moments counted for something.

Quite frankly, their argument was ridiculous. The fact that it had split up their long-standing friendship made it even more ludicrous. Everyone knew it—including them. Yet instead of facing the truth about themselves, they kept up the effort to make the colors of the church nursery the wedge that drove apart their relationship for three decades.

Isn't the length we'll go to in order to avoid the truth about ourselves simply amazing sometimes?

You'll be pleased to know that Hilda got better and is presently enjoying a renewed friendship with Marian. But with that happy ending, let's not lose the lesson of their story. For thirty years, both Hilda and Marian were bothered by the loss of their relationship. But they were afraid to face the truth that their feud made them look silly to those around them. Each one knew that reconciliation would mean facing her own pettiness. To avoid that painful truth, they avoided each other.

Face it: We're not so different. Which of us *doesn't* choose to avoid pain when possible—even the pain of the truth? Facing the pain of who we truly are, of the honest results of our actions, is a key to maintaining—or rebuilding—trust in any relationship. Marian's question at the end of her hospital conversation with Hilda was serious. It affirmed that the friends had been reconciled, and that trust was being reestablished between them. "This still counts" meant that the two had faced the truth about themselves, painful as it was, and were willing to continue their relationship based on mutual trust.

But never forget this undeniable characteristic of truth: Sometimes it hurts. In those instances, it takes courage to face the pain. Recently, we learned of two friends—let's call them Lon and Ken—who were suffering through a broken relationship. They agreed that it would be right and healthy for them to talk about what was going on between them. Devlin won the opportunity to mediate the discussion.

Lon was ready to make things right. That meant owning up to his part in the rift just as truthfully as discussing how he'd been hurt in the process. He delivered marvelously. He was open, honest, and conciliatory.

In contrast, Ken had come simply to offer a litany of wrongs he'd suffered at Lon's hands.

Need we say the session didn't make it very far down the pathway of reconciliation? Later, Lon talked with Devlin about his frustration. He'd come to the session willing to be honest about himself and the relationship, only to have Ken offer an inventory of grievous wrongs—with no admission of responsibility for the breakdown in the relationship. It was painfully apparent that Ken was eager to share all of his pain, but unwilling to look at his own behavior.

Lon mentioned that at least he had a clear conscience about the meeting. He felt good about his effort to hear and accept the truth about the pain his own actions had caused. Yet there was no question that the issue wasn't resolved to his satisfaction. What made Ken unable, unwilling, or powerless to face the truth about his own actions?

It's the problem of pain—the painful truth.

Contrast Ken's behavior with that of Richard. As a young man, Richard found out that putting a college degree on his résumé increased his chances of getting a job. It wasn't like he'd *never* attended college—he just didn't have a degree attached to the experience.

Richard was a voracious reader. He also learned more from being on the job than he could have ever garnered from a classroom. It wasn't long until he was in an up-and-coming company—with the "fudge factor" still in his résumé. A promotion soon followed. A few years later, his work habits earned him another promotion—and he suddenly found himself on the executive track.

The résumé issue was nearly forgotten until one day in an executives' session. The president of the company stood up and announced, "We're on our way to the Fortune 500 ranks. We need to start putting our ducks in a row.

"That's why I'm asking you all to look at another degree. Some of you need to track for an MBA, others for doctorates in your respective fields. We need to set the example for the rest of the company. We'll give you the time you need for the necessary class work. And the tuition bill is on the company."

Richard sat resolutely through the rest of the meeting. When the session was over, he caught the president's eye. "I need to talk to you."

They waited for the others to leave the room, then shut the door behind them. Richard wasted no time and minced no words. "You need to know that I don't even have a bachelor's degree. And it was deliberate misrepresentation on my part when I applied to work here ten years ago. My résumé says I have a degree. In all honesty, I haven't thought much about it since I filled out the application.

"I don't want to cause you any embarrassment, so I'll resign if you'll let me."

The president swallowed hard. "Richard, you know the drill here. I can't let you off the hook. You had a chance to come clean every time you were promoted and the job requirements paragraph said 'a four-year undergraduate degree.'"

"I know. I wish I could change it now, but I can't."

"I'll accept your resignation. But I want you to do me a favor."

"What's that?"

"Get your degree. In the meantime, let me use you as a consultant now and then. I'll even write you a recommendation to take around to other companies. You don't have to lie about your impact here—it's been great. But the integrity issue, I just can't ignore."

Richard went home that day and told his wife the news. It wasn't the most happy moment of their marriage, either. But it was a watershed day for Richard. By facing the truth about himself, he began a process of healing. His self-esteem actually improved because he didn't have to hide behind a lie to prove his worth in his field of expertise.

Things were tight financially for Richard and his family for a while, but he managed. Richard became a consultant. Eventually, he not only received his undergraduate degree, but also a master's degree. Now he happily consults for businesses and teaches at a community college.

Richard faced the painful truth and resolved a past issue that would have haunted him the rest of his career.

Turning the Question on Ourselves

We have a tendency to project our personal ills on society sometimes. Just as likely, society reflects the sum total of those personal ills. So when we saw the Barna survey that asked how society was doing in the categories of "honesty and integrity" as compared with ten years ago, we were intrigued to discover that just over half of us believed that things were getting worse. About one-third of us believed things were staying the same, while 10 percent of us actually believed honesty and integrity were faring better.[1]

A majority of us sees truth in deterioration. Do you think that could be because we wonder how well it's doing in our personal lives?

Why is speaking the truth so important in all aspects of life? Our perspective is that the truth can be seen as the great equalizer. If we're free to accept the truth about ourselves, then it's much easier to accept the shortcomings of others. Truth can be the great healer if we allow it to be. It can expose those areas within each of us that are selfish, vindictive, inconsiderate, dark, and evil.

Truth is the one principle that allows us to see ourselves—and our situations—honestly. Truth provides the moment of decision when each of us can decide to change who we are, what we are, and what we do. When we apply the Rule of Truth—being honest with ourselves before we point out the truth in others—something amazing often happens. What we find in ourselves is remarkably similar to what we feel so compelled to point out to others.

The discovery that we are as flawed as those we want to critique is painful to face. It can bring about a different reaction to that "moment of truth": a response of profound inaction to the truth.

Why? When faced with truth about ourselves, most of us become defensive. Sometimes that response is an attempt to ease the pain of seeing ourselves just as we are. Other times it's a guard against seeing the sad results of the things we have done.

Our friend Paul has quite a temper sometimes. When his temper gets the best of him, his response is to verbally abuse the air around him. His wife, Tricia, called him on this habit more than once. Paul's response was consistent: "Oh, come on, it's not that big a deal. Better that I throw around language than chairs, right?"

But not long ago, Paul overheard his five-year-old son delivering some choice words in the family room. He ran to see what was going on, and found his son ranting and raving at a video game controller that wasn't performing to his expectations.

Paul was quick with a reprimand. Then he followed up with a question: "Son, wherever did you hear that sort of language?"

The lad was unhesitating in his response: "I just said what *you* say, Dad."

Paul immediately went on the defensive. "Now, son, when did you hear me *ever* use that kind of language?"

Again, an unhesitating response followed: "Whenever the lawn mower doesn't work the way you want it to, that's what you say."

Paul was taken aback for a moment. Then he had to nod his head. "I guess we *both* have to work on our language, don't we?"

Paul has discovered the impact his words have on innocent bystanders. It will take some time before this habit will break. In the meantime, Paul is left with the results of this blind spot in his own character that is now reflected in his son—and he wishes that he'd faced the truth about his language habits much sooner.

Emotional Leprosy

But let's not be too hard on Paul. Part of human nature is the reflex to protect ourselves from pain. Yet pain plays an essential and vital role in our lives. From a medical standpoint, its purpose is actually to keep us from further harm.

For generations, people believed leprosy was a malady that caused the decay and deterioration of an individual's flesh. But modern science has determined that, in addition to causing this decay, leprosy actually deadens one's nerves. Then, as the nerves deaden, an individual harms himself without knowing it. The result? Someone stricken with leprosy is far more prone to suffer lacerations or puncture wounds *without even knowing it.*

These unfelt injuries lead to the neglect of the wound. In turn, that neglect leads to horrible infections. These infections are one of the visible effects of the disease—they were once thought to be the primary symptom of the disease.

Watch this process: As someone with leprosy loses feeling, he's at risk for a variety of secondary afflictions, which can quickly escalate into life-threatening difficulties.

Still want a life without pain? The truth is that pain, while uncomfortable, unpleasant, and generally distressing, is the alarm system that tells us something is wrong.

In our culture, we've made the avoidance of pain an art form. We want pain relief first and above anything else. This is certainly true physically—and what is true in reference to our bodies is just as true in reference to our character.

We want to avoid emotional and psychic pain to an even greater degree. We are people who look to avoid any truth about ourselves that might be emotionally unpleasant; we play emotional lepers. The result is that we begin to deaden our nerves to things that are not functioning correctly. Our character, our personality, and our spirit begin to decay.

The consequence of truthfulness (or lack thereof) goes far deeper than the simple (and highly valid) arguments of "it's wrong to lie" or "deception is evil." The more dire consequence of not telling or facing the truth is that we start down a path that fosters the decay of our conscience and the decomposition of our character, both individually and corporately. The more we work to avoid pain in order to feel good, the sicker we make ourselves, and the more gangrenous our spirits and diseased our personalities become.

In a culture obsessed with health, both physical and mental, we have apparently redefined the health of our character. "Health" seems to mean the absence of any pain. Health in relationships and in our own personal mental and spiritual beings is no longer defined in terms of optimum function or well-being. Instead, we've bought the premise that to be pain-free is to be healthy.

That's dangerous. Without pain, maladies that are treatable—actually possible to heal—become life threatening.

So we're led to what may be the "million-dollar question" of this book: *What is so frightening about healthy truth-telling that we'll live in a way to avoid its pain at all costs?*

Getting Healthy with the Truth

Not long ago, Steve received permission to lift weights again as part of his physical workout. What makes that significant? For several years, Steve has been treated for mild hypertension. The common wisdom was that doing circuit training with weights, even light weights (Steve's not about to head for the Olympics anytime soon), would be counterproductive for the treatment of his hypertension.

Steve's bout with hypertension came after several lousy blood-pressure readings at successive appointments with the doctor almost a decade ago. As is often the case with high blood pressure, there were no obvious symptoms. In fact, the readings always came as the result of other reasons to visit the doctor. Steve never went to the doctor looking for the truth about his blood pressure. But the readings wouldn't go away, either.

Hold that thought while we talk about this: The most common way of avoiding pain is never to allow yourself to be in a position where someone might feel comfortable sharing with you truthfully. In Steve's case, that meant avoiding the doctor's office and anyone with a blood-pressure cuff, if at all possible. He never really "felt" his hypertension, after all. But he struggled with the truth of the readings, and the fact that he needed to deal with the problem *before* it began showing obvious symptoms.

A slightly less common way of avoiding pain is our continued lifestyle of denial when clearly confronted with issues about ourselves. Even in the face of overwhelming and incontrovertible evidence, we'll use every slight of hand or manipulation—and more times than we like to admit, outright aggression—to keep us from learning the truth about ourselves. For some months Steve had a problem admitting to himself that he had hypertension. His wife, Annie, was well aware of it, as was a close circle of friends. For them, Steve would say, "Yep, we have to work on this blood pressure thing." But to himself? "Can it really be hypertension? I wonder if it's just a spike on this isolated reading because of work . . . or the next deadline . . . or those pounds I packed on at Christmas . . . or . . . "

The work that lies before us is to create a personal context where we understand that the pain of the truth about ourselves, while uncomfortable, is not debilitating. It is, in fact, liberating. Truth is light that dispels the fear of secrets. Truth allows us to avoid that thickening knot in our stomachs when we think about all the things we're hiding and to avoid the fear that grows from the idea that we might actually be exposed to others. The façade that we believe *protects* us actually only *shields* us from pain. It enables us to continue on with great gusto being the natural-born people we want to be. But it doesn't allow us to work on becoming the people that, deep in our hearts, we know we would like to become.

For Steve, the truth was that he wanted to be in control of his hypertension. The first thing to do was to face the truth of his situation: "I have hypertension." No embellishments, no excuses, just ownership of the problem.

The second thing to do was to look forward to the truth about his problem rather than avoid the truth about it. That means a consistent monitoring of his blood pressure at home and at the doctor's office. But don't miss this: *At that point, truth became Steve's liberator rather than debilitator.*

The third thing to do was to take action to make it better. Steve hates taking pills. But he's faithful with his medication. And because he hates taking pills, instead of increasing the dosage of the medication, Steve works with his doctor to take more active, alternative steps against hypertension: karate, basketball, diet adjustments, and now light circuit weight training. His goal is to become the poster child for recovering hypertensives. According to his last few trips to the doctor, he just might make it.

The Pilgrimage and the Paradox

All that being said, it took Steve almost seven years to get to this point. How long might it take to work on a character issue? It's usually easier to deal with a highly objective measure of truth like a weight scale or a blood-pressure reading than it is to deal with a character reading. Yet those character readings are what constantly measure the integrity of our everyday pilgrimage.

That leaves us with the personal paradox we face when talking about the impact of truth. On the one hand, the pain of facing the truth about ourselves is real. There's no question about it. On the other hand, once we begin to accept the truth about ourselves we become far more comfortable with who we are—and what our real problems are. At that point, further revelations about ourselves, while still painful, are easier to accept. And in accepting ourselves and our challenges alike, we're liberated to become more fully who we should be.

There's a section of the song "An Apology" by the group Hangnail (we're not kidding) that seems to boil down the basic human reaction to truth:

It's hard to take the blame
But sometimes credit's due
It's easier to rearrange
What's wrong from what is true.[2]

Facing the truth about ourselves is worth the pain. So should we go searching for pain? Are we like the monks of times past that wore hair shirts and flogged themselves so they could know continual suffering? You can do what you want, but for us the answer is no. So should we avoid all pain to live a "happy" life? Again, the answer is no.

Real feeling is not a static experience. It's dynamic. Think about it: when have you experienced one single feeling? More often than not, when one feeling becomes more real, so do others. And the *kinds* of feelings that join together may not always seem to match at first. This is one of those instances.

Ultimately, we experience more joy when we face our pain, recognize its source, and begin the process of healing. Pain allows us to see our shortcomings. When we embrace who we are—warts, scars, blisters, and all—something amazing begins to happen. An honest assessment of our flaws and challenges can lead us to viable action to deal with them. Then those things within us that we fear, those things that we don't want anyone else to see, lose their power.

Once we've determined to see truth as our liberator—not our captor—we no longer need to fear what we'll see in the light of truth.

section two

embracing truth in a culture of lies

truth and spirituality truth and spirituality truth and spirituality truth and spirituality truth and spirituality truth and spirituality truth and spirituality truth and spirituality truth and spirituality truth and spirituality truth and spirituality truth and sp

Chapter

4 ▶ truth and spirituality

Talk to me about the truth of religion and I'll listen gladly. Talk to me about the duty of religion and I'll listen submissively. But don't come talking to me about the consolations of religion or I shall suspect that you don't understand.
—C. S. Lewis

Evan had gone to live with his grandfather, Ned, in Maine. Ned lived in an old captain's house overlooking the ocean. When Evan wasn't in school, he and Ned spent long hours together beachcombing. They gathered driftwood that intrigued them and picked up agate that had been worn to contrasting stripes. But most of all, they enjoyed each other's company.

Before you think this sounds too idyllic, you need to know this: Evan was with Ned because his parents had been killed in a head-on crash with a drunk driver. Even though his parents' will had placed him with his mother's sister, everyone in the family agreed that Evan needed some time away—some quiet time—to work through his grief. Ned, Evan's paternal grandfather, was the perfect person to help Evan, and he happily took on the task.

It took several weeks of walking in near silence before Evan began opening up, even to his beloved "Grampy." There were times when those journeys would end with the fifteen-year-old suddenly turning to his grandfather's shoulder and choking out sobs. Nothing verbal, just anguish.

And that would be the end of the day's walk. But Ned knew it was enough.

Time passed. Ned avoided yielding to the temptations to liken his grandson's situation to the ongoing rhythm of the tides, the vast expanse of the ocean, the glowing horizon at sunrise. He simply listened and waited. Eventually, Evan began attending church with Ned. He even began to participate on the fringe of the activities that the church had for kids. But one Sunday evening, Evan exploded through the kitchen door in a rage.

"Grampy, that's it! I've had it with church! I just don't believe the part where they keep telling me 'God works all things together for good.' What's with that, anyway? It's pretty stinking easy for someone else to tell me everything's working out all right when they have parents to go home to!"

It was the moment Ned had been anticipating—not that it made it any easier. Ned stayed quiet for a few seconds to make sure Evan was through with his outburst. Yet even before Ned gathered his thoughts to speak, Evan was already backpedaling a bit.

"Grampy, that may have not sounded the way it should have. I want to be here with you now, it's just that . . . "

"Don't worry about it, buddy. Don't worry about it at all. I know what you mean. People usually mean well when they say that about God making something good out of the bad. It doesn't always come across that way, that's all."

Ned pointed to a small china cabinet in the corner of the dining room. He put his hand on Evan's shoulder, and gently guided him to the cabinet. On the top shelf was an oyster shell, shellacked in an open position. In its lower half rested a pearl—beautiful, if imperfect.

"Remember where that pearl came from, buddy?"

"Sure, Grampy. The Sea of Japan, when you worked over there as a diver for a salvage company. That's one of my favorite things you have."

"Mine, too. But you know something? People think that pearl is beautiful, right? Know how it happened? A lot of time, a lot of pressure, and a whole lot of irritation. A grain of sand gets lodged inside an oyster, and it gets irritated. It secretes something to protect itself from the irritation, and keeps being irritated, and keeps secreting stuff, and finally there's a pearl. Looks beautiful to us, but it's just a major pain to the oyster.

"Some people think that when God does something beautiful it's like going on a vacation to some fancy resort. You get pampered, you get primed, and you walk away ready to be on television. I've never seen it work that way.

"While you're figuring out what God has for you, you spend a lot of time being irritated. You get put into a pressure cooker that would make the toughest clams melt like butter. You stay there longer than you want to. And about the time you're ready to blow up or collapse, you just might figure out that God has done something special—something beautiful in the long run—that keeps you sane.

"Buddy, the best I can tell you is that with time, with the pressure, the pain, and the irritation, comes growth. I hate the price you're paying to grow like this. God knows I'd change it if I could—but I can't. All I can tell you is, I believe God weeps when we do. The psalms say so. And I'll be here for you as long as God allows, too.

"And maybe someday, we'll figure *something* out that makes some sense out of all this."

The Wild Truth

You'll notice that Ned completely refused to use spirituality to help Evan dodge the truth about his situation. Instead, Ned used spirituality to provide his grandson a context for dealing with the truth.

How does spirituality affect our perspective on truth, anyway? Nearly two-thirds of teenagers who identified themselves as having an orthodox view of God considered "living with a high degree of integrity" as being "very desirable" for their lives compared with 55 percent of those who identified themselves as not having an orthodox view of God.[1] Among adults, those who identified themselves as having some kind of Christian affiliation consistently scored themselves higher in keeping the commandment that says "Do not lie" than those who identified themselves as being outside the Christian faith.[2]

At least on the surface, then, those with a defined spirituality seem to appreciate and practice the truth a bit more consistently than those without such spirituality. Of course, the possibility exists that those people may be lying to themselves about their priorities and practices.

Another possibility is that the truth is not as easily attained as it is admired.

In the recent box-office smash *The Matrix*, Keanu Reeves plays a reluctant savior for mankind. In order to be in a position to fulfill his destiny, Reeves' character,

Neo, is taught and molded by a character called Morpheus. When struggling with one particular lesson, Morpheus challenges Neo by saying, "There is a difference between knowing the path and walking the path."[3]

That single sentence sums up the challenges that we face individually, as families, and as a culture. Virtually every system of belief attached to spirituality will acknowledge the importance of truth-telling, the value of honesty, and the need for integrity in communication. Yet as a people, just over 70 percent of us agree to some degree with the following statement: "When it comes to morals and ethics, what is right and wrong, there are no absolute standards that apply to everybody in all situations." However, professed spirituality profoundly reduces the percentage of those agreeing with the statement.[4] The point here? Faith increases the likelihood that we'll embrace absolutes.

It seems, then, that in part we use spirituality to help us identify the ideals we'll aspire to. We use spirituality to affirm that those ideals have value. This is true for Christians, Jews, Muslims, Hindus, and Buddhists alike. We all teach our children, for example, that telling the truth is very important. In fact, if you ever have the chance to observe parents when their child tells them a lie, you'll hear a conversation (make that "a parental monologue") that is nearly universal. It may contain different words, but the ideas generally go something like this: "Don't lie to me. You must tell the truth. Telling the truth is very important." At least in our children, then, we want the ideal of truth to produce a practical application of truth.

How else does spirituality impact truth? Perhaps, as in the case of Ned and his grandson, Evan, it also provides a context for the truth to be applied to our everyday lives—and it begins the application with us. The big question, then, is this: how do we move from *knowing* that the path of truth is the right path to actually *walking* the right path, or living a life that is distinguished by truth-telling?

For knowing which road to take, as Morpheus so clearly states to Neo, is not the same as *living* and *walking* on the right road.

Knowing, Living, and a Starting Point

We believe that the place where a person begins not simply to *know* but actually to *live* the truthful life is in the spiritual journey.

The irony is that while spiritual development has become a very popular subject, putting the principles of these spiritual paths into everyday action is another matter. Our culture seems to believe that compiling a lot of information about spirituality from books, support groups, book-of-the-month interest groups, and churches is enough in itself. Our society has bought into the notion that knowledge without obedience is complete enough to realize the benefits of a growing spirituality.

Each of the major world religions places a significant emphasis on truth-telling. So what makes it so difficult for the practitioners of these religions to live out the truth-telling obligations of their faith? Could a modern fallacy be choking out the value of truth in our spiritual lives? This fallacy tells us that everything taught in a religion is unattainable today, in the here and now—that the destination is the important thing and that the journey is a necessary evil to be endured until we realize our reward.

"I can't wait to grow up!" is a constant cry of Steve's daughter, Maggie. Her world has been filled with the desire to cook on her own, fix her hair on her own, decorate her room on her own, and . . . well, you get the picture. Maggie began asking for the keys to the family car when she was three. It hasn't let up since.

But at this writing, as Maggie approaches her ninth birthday, the reality check of that cry comes in a moment of genuine injury. Then, if Steve is around, Maggie becomes "Daddy's girl" all over again while they clean the skinned knee and reach for the Band-Aids. Another reality check comes when Maggie realizes that, as bright as she is, she doesn't know how to fix a favorite toy that has fallen apart. In both instances, she's confronted with the truth that she needs to grow up more, to gain more experience and knowledge—and to take the time to do it.

In a world of instant gratification, the idea that growth and development— physical, spiritual, and social alike—take time and effort is an affront to us. Like an impatient child, we want spiritual maturity, spiritual strength, and spiritual wisdom *now.* Why should we have to suffer through the time, energy, mistakes, and scars that experience will bring? Can't we just bypass the pain (ah, that word again) and struggle of the process, and earn our maturity and wisdom in the abstract?

This attitude proves that there's one thing we rarely take into consideration: Truth-telling is a large concept—a universal one, we believe—and learning how to use truth as a positive force is a huge undertaking. From a spiritual standpoint, truth-telling is about taking eternal principles and figuring out how to wisely apply them in a distorted, temporal world. It takes time both to learn and to apply. No instant gratification here!

So how do we embark on this journey of growth into truth-telling? How can spirituality help us develop the strength of character to live truth-telling lives? Let's look at it this way: Our spiritual journey needs to begin at home. *Our spiritual journey starts with how we view ourselves.*

At this point, of course, the patterns of spiritual journeys become wildly divergent. Some people look at themselves and simply don't see (or want to see) anything in themselves that is not as it should be. Then there are those who recognize the fact that none of us is perfect. In fact, upon reflection we don't even meet our *own* expectations—much less any outside standard.

Orthodoxy only goes so far in this area. Even if we agree intellectually with what a faith system teaches about the nature and destiny of humankind, there's no guarantee we'll apply that to ourselves. But if we allow it to, a healthy spiritual life will help us to take a more objective view of ourselves. It will help us deal with the fact that we're neither perfect nor worthless. It can—and should—be an indispensable tool in applying the Rule of Truth.

We should be up-front here and tell you that we are Christians. Our views on spirituality are certainly colored by our own faith journeys. Still, let's look at an example of others whose experience might help us understand the process that is necessary to be a growing, healthy spiritual person.

Hi, I'm _____, and I'm a Recovering Liar

We have a number of friends who are recovering alcoholics or drug abusers. They'll often talk about their experiences with Alcoholics Anonymous, Cocaine Anonymous, or Narcotics Anonymous. These groups have given them their most reality-based and practical help.

We're in no way experts in the twelve-step programs. Yet as we reviewed the twelve steps employed in some way in each of the above programs, we were taken with how firmly and deeply rooted each one is in the idea of telling the truth. Each step demands truth-telling, first to yourself and then to others.

Step 1 is to acknowledge that you have no power, none at all, over the addiction. That's right: You make a truthful admission of your powerlessness regarding your addiction. Only then do you create the environment where you can actually gain the right kind of power to deal with it.

That seems to be a paradox, doesn't it? Yet nearly any recovering alcoholic or addict will tell you, with a great degree of passion, that until you are honest with yourself and accept your powerlessness, you'll never gain any victory over a life-controlling addiction. Until you've reached the place where you can honestly admit your weakness and powerlessness, you're doomed to continue to struggle. And one more thing: they'll tell you that it's pride that keeps individuals from making this crucial admission.

Another of the twelve steps is about making amends. This entire step is about looking honestly at what you've been willing to do—to yourself and to others—to continue in your addiction. A careful and honest examination of your behavior will lead you to a place where you can offer your apologies and your admissions of guilt to those you have hurt. This is truth-telling: honestly reflecting on yourself and telling yourself the truth about who you are and what your actions have done. As painful and disturbing as this process is, it's the very thing that makes healing possible.

There are few, if any, easy steps among the twelve steps. They demand an individual's ruthless self-examination, glaring honesty about her actions (and inaction), and painful encounters with those the individual has deeply wounded.

Why are we spending so much time dealing with twelve-step programs and addictions? Simple. Those who have dealt with an alcoholic or addict will tell you that one of the fundamental symptoms of that person's condition is lying. Addicts and alcoholics become champions of lying, deceit, misdirection, and manipulation. The physical result of their diseases is the destruction of the body. The spiritual result of their diseases is the destruction of the very values that allow for healthy relationships. Their condition always results in relationships broken by lies and deceit. Healing only comes after being honest with themselves, which sets them on a path of recovery from the emotional leprosy they had fallen victim to during their addictions.

We contend, however, that these steps are not simply for those who struggle with alcohol and drugs. The truth of the twelve steps is not at all unlike the Rule of Truth we discussed in chapter 2: In order to take part in the process of helping others by pointing out their shortcomings, we must first qualify ourselves by applying the same standard to ourselves. We have to enter into this realm of truth-telling with the classic admission, "Hi! I'm (put your name here), and I'm a recovering liar."

Only then can we move on.

Honesty Can Be Ruthless

In most addiction recovery programs, you'll find a ruthless honesty put into practice by the leaders to benefit new attendees who aren't being truthful. They won't allow any self-deception, manipulation, or self-serving ideas from the newcomers. However, once someone has been honest with them about his story and situation, nothing that person can say will bring condemnation. Honesty is rewarded by acceptance. The pain is tempered by love.

Wouldn't it be wonderful if those of us proclaiming a spiritual basis for life would extend that same kind of love and acceptance to those who practice honesty? Instead, we too often use spirituality as an excuse to exclude those who have shortcomings we can't accept.

It's an amazing thing to see a religious community react to a member who has fallen short of the community ethic. Thirty years ago, Jack was a junior in high school. He had a one-night encounter with a prom date. She ended up pregnant, eventually giving the child up for adoption. She moved out of their small town, never to return.

Jack, on the other hand, stayed there. He joined the National Guard and served well there. He threw himself into church activities after he graduated from high school. He made a commitment to Christ that completely changed his life. He served as an usher. He played on the church softball team. He sang in the choir.

But, even after he went to college and received his degree to teach high school, Jack's hometown church never let him teach Sunday school. There was one old saint on the Christian Education board who couldn't let go of the fact that Jack "had gotten a girl pregnant." It didn't matter that Jack had confessed the sin, and even openly discussed with the youth in the church the heartbreak he had caused. It didn't matter that the event was at least a decade past. It didn't matter that Jack was happily married with two growing children at home. *It just didn't matter.*

To Jack's credit, he considers to this day that being honest about his failure is its own reward. He didn't teach Sunday school until just a few years back. But he slept with a clear conscience because he accepted, and dealt with, the truth about himself.

And the old saint? At her funeral ten years ago, her daughter Adele introduced a stranger to the church. "This is my half-brother, Nick. Mom gave him up for adoption before she met Dad."

All those years, and nobody in the church knew.

What about ourselves? Isn't a spiritual journey absent of honest self-examination usually a journey toward self-gratification more than a journey toward self-realization? And doesn't that self-gratification too often come needlessly at the expense of others?

Pushing Through the Pain

A friend of ours who serves as a campus chaplain at a large university told us the story of Vince who, all through college, enjoyed poking fun at "those poor pagans" who were caught up in the "awful vice of smoking cigarettes." Vince loved railing on anyone within his sight who lit up. He knew all the latest facts about the damage cigarettes could do to vital organs. He even confronted strangers with those facts as part of what he perceived to be his "Christian duty."

Problem was, even in college Vince had a pretty ample waistline. The campus pastor caught him haranguing a smoker outside the student union one day while he gnawed his way through not one, not two, but three cheese Danishes. When the pastor approached Vince and the smoker, Vince thought he was about to gain an ally to change the heathen smoker's errant ways.

You should have seen Vince's face when the campus pastor took him by the elbow and moved him away as he said to the smoker, "Excuse us, please." Then the pastor whispered through his teeth, "Enough is enough. Before you say *anything* else to *anyone* about smoking, you lose thirty pounds. *Period.*"

Vince soon discovered that his addiction to food was just as crippling a problem—and probably as dangerous to his health—as smoking. He was devastated as he came face to face with his own lack of discipline. The belief system that he thought would continue to support his self-gratification wouldn't. Self-examination was much harder than he'd expected.

But there's another Vince we'd like to call to your attention. Vince Lombardi, the former coach of the Green Bay Packers, is still well known for his disciplinarian approach to the game. Lombardi knew that pain played an integral part in preparing his players for success. He prepared them for pain—to know it, to play through it. He worked them very hard. Only then did they discover their true limitations, not some limitation that they put upon themselves at the first blush of pain. Lombardi knew that the more he could push his players, the more they would find themselves capable of doing in the game.

Are we so different from those players? In our spiritual journeys, the more we discover about who we really are, the more we can learn what our true limitations are. Then we can live in that paradox where we actually find freedom by knowing what our limitations are.

This same principle applies to truth-telling behavior. Once we know our own limitations as people, as spiritual beings, we'll find that we handle the truth about others in a far more forgiving way.

This isn't some principle that applies only to people who profess religious faith in Christ. Let's assume that in your own journey you are trying to figure out just who or what God might be. In that journey of knowing who God is, you'll begin to discover who you are and who you're not.

Isn't that, after all, one of the points of the journey: to understand who we are and who we're not? So how can we look at our lives and improve them, make them more godly or more full of good and positive action, unless we look closely and carefully at the reality of who we are?

Positive spirituality can supply the context for doing just that. It won't deny us the truth, but rather will help us make the best use of it. Therefore, it comes with this warning: You may not feel consoled in the process of discovering the truth about—or telling the truth to—yourself. But the end result will prove to you that you *do* understand at least one important thing spirituality should do: impact your everyday life.

the response to truth the response to truth the
response to truth the response to truth the response to
truth the response to truth the response to truth the
response to truth the response to truth the response to
truth the response to truth the response to truth the
response to truth the response to truth the response to
truth the response to truth the response to truth the

Chapter

5 ▶ the response to truth

The weakness of a soul is proportionate to the number of truths that must be kept from it.
—Eric Hoffer

We have a love-hate relationship with the scene in the movie *A Christmas Story* where Ralphie, the elementary-school hero, slips up and swears. He ends up getting his mouth washed out with soap.

Why the love-hate feeling? Because we've had up-close-and-personal experiences with the same. And we share a family tradition with soap applied to one's mouth.

Usually the "reward" of having a bar of Ivory or, heaven help you, Lifebuoy (writer Jean Shepard wasn't kidding in *A Christmas Story)* suddenly in contact with your taste buds was a result of bad language. That's the classic example. But in our families, you could also get your mouth washed out with soap for telling a lie.

We again defer to Steve's experience in this area. There's a near-legendary account of his telling a lie that still has them talking in southwest Iowa. Heaven knows what he was thinking at the tender age of six on that Saturday night so long ago. . . .

Steve shared a bedroom with two older brothers growing up. In fact, they were in high school when Steve was just beginning his elementary-school years. That means they had a lot of cool stuff on their dressers that Steve wasn't supposed to touch.

But hey—it was a Saturday night, they were at a school dance, and Steve was bored. So he walked over to one of their dressers. There was a brightly colored tube of hair cream on the dresser, used only once when Steve's brother Jim prepared his locks for the dance.

This was new, highly advertised stuff that Steve had seen on TV commercials. If it worked for Jim, maybe it would work for him. So he unscrewed the tube's cap and gave it a little squeeze. Steve took the cream that came out, rubbed it in both hands, smeared it on his hair, and reached back up on the dresser to use Jim's hairbrush.

That's when he noticed the tube had not stopped delivering the hair cream. In fact, the hair cream was pulsing out of that tube as though it had a life of its own. Not realizing that he needed to equalize the pressure inside and outside the tube, Steve simply screwed the lid back on the tube—and watched as the hair cream pushed it back off again.

Steve squeezed that tube into a variety of shapes in the next few seconds. One such effort finally halted the flow of hair cream. But by that time, some of it had actually made it off the cloth that covered the dresser top to the wood around the edges.

But the night's work was not yet done. Steve turned and noticed a camera on his brother Don's dresser. The flash bulb even seemed to be intact. Wouldn't it be cool to play photographer for a while, like Don, who was a photographer for the high-school yearbook?

Of course it would! So Steve reached for the camera, hoping to have a chance to pretend to be a photographer with a real camera. With the lens and flash unit pointed toward him, Steve attempted the grab. The lens triggered, the camera flashed, and Steve's dad noticed the flash from the hallway.

"Son, what are you up to?"

"Oh, nuthin'."

"Well then, let's see what *nuthin'* looks like."

The evidence in the room should have been enough to convince Steve to drop any pretense of innocence. But panic set in, overtaking reason in Steve's mind.

Steve's dad raised an eyebrow as he looked at the camera. "The flash just fired on this camera, Steve. The bulb's still hot. Do you know anything about that?"

"Well . . . uhh . . . "

"Yes or no, son."

"Sort of."

"Right. And there's a big mess over on Jim's dresser, and your hair looks nice and slicked over. Any ideas?"

"I don't know, Dad."

"But I think you do."

"Well, okay, but I don't know how it happened. That tube just kept spitting out the hair stuff, and I just wanted to play with Don's camera for a while, and . . . "

"But son, you're not supposed to touch your brothers' things."

"Well, it wasn't exactly *touching*. It was kind of *borrowing*."

"Did you ask if you could do that?"

"Well . . . " It was then that Steve saw an avenue of escape. "I thought I did."

It bought Steve about two more hours. His brothers came home, they denied (truthfully so) ever having discussed such permission, and Steve's minute-long encounter with Ivory began.

To this day, Steve still believes it to be an act of mercy that his dad used the soap from the upstairs bathroom instead of the downstairs shower. But he could have dodged the soap completely if he'd just faced the truth in the first place and developed a proper *response* instead of a panicked *reaction*.

In any case, the event helped Steve develop a taste for truth.

Response Versus Reaction

When you talk about the truth, what do you talk about? Do you focus on the nature of truth? Do you bring up personal examples of pain and betrayal from truth-telling or hearing the truth? Do you manufacture situations defined by exceptional circumstances to exempt yourself from the responsibility of being truthful in your own situation?

These questions have a common factor: They deflect the discussion about telling the truth. But we find ourselves pursuing those tangents because they move the discussion away from ourselves. They give us permission to speculate on how another person in another situation should respond to the truth. And we can artfully dodge facing our own response to the truth.

Often, what's most important to us about the truth is championing its importance, not dealing with its very real impact. Talking about the truth is easier than telling the truth. Telling the truth can be easier than hearing it, too. So in our response to the truth we must keep in mind these things: *Telling the truth is only part of the equation that we face as humans. Hearing the truth and responding to it in healthy and constructive ways is at least as important.*

Please don't miss the importance of *response*. If we simply *react* to the truth, it's likely we'll form a judgment about that truth that helps us bypass it. But if we *respond* to the truth responsibly, we'll assess the information and take appropriate action.

Martial artists tell stories to teach the difference between a reaction and a response. One such story exists in several different systems of martial arts training.[1] Once there was an instructor who wished to evaluate his students' progress. He set up a simple test for the evaluation: A valuable porcelain teacup was balanced on the upper edge of a slightly opened door. As each student came into the room, they would "encounter" the cup on its way to the floor.

The first student was a beginner. He had enough skills to hurt someone, but not a lot of control. So when he came through the doorway, his instructor watched as the cup hit him. He was quick enough to catch the cup and move it to a far corner of the room before it could do him, or anyone else, any further injury. It was a reaction of self-preservation, but little more.

This is the same kind of reaction we have whenever we encounter the truth and perceive it as a threat. Our reaction, usually charged with emotion, is to remove—or run from—the thing that could cause us further pain. We'll do away with the "truth encounter" in exchange for our perceived safety.

The second student was more advanced. When she entered the doorway, she noticed the cup falling and caught it. Looking it over, she saw what it was and smiled. She then presented it to her instructors. "This looks valuable. You should have it," she said. She reacted well, and responded according to the reality of what she saw.

In a similar way, an encounter with truth can look like a threat at first. But if you catch what you can out of the encounter, you'll preserve the lesson and learn from it. Then you can develop an even better response based on what you caught.

The story doesn't end there. There was yet another student, almost ready to become an instructor himself. This student was ready for a test. He'd learned from experience to watch for situations that could teach him something. As he came to the doorway, he noticed the door was slightly ajar. He stopped in his tracks and examined the situation. He saw the porcelain cup on top of the door and recognized it as one from his instructor's favorite tea set. Rather than risk breaking the cup, this student went around to another entrance. He approached the door from the inside, carefully removed the cup from its perch, turned to his instructor, and asked, "May I prepare you some tea?"

This is like a mature response to the truth. Experience can teach us to look for the treasure—the truth—at every turn. It can also prove that the truth should be handled with great care. In other words, the more you know the value of the truth—and the more you encounter it—the more truth can serve you and others around you.

Responses to Truth Encounters: The Blizzard of Id

Here's a key to shatter the numbness of our emotional leprosy: Work on a healthy response to the truth, however painful it might be. Remember that twisted logic can cause us to believe that the absence of all pain—even the pain of the truth—is healthy.

Let's start here. We believe strongly that the truth doesn't necessarily evoke the same reaction from individual to individual. In fact, the truth likely won't evoke the same reaction from the same individual if the time, circumstances, and emotional status of that individual differ from situation to situation. So there are really two responses to truth in every relational transaction.

The first is the emotional, natural response. In Freudian terms you might want to view it as the "id" response. In nonFreudian terms, it's a reflex—a reflex of unbridled emotion that is basically self-centered. The second could be called the "cerebral" or (if you want to take a trip down the Freudian lane again) "super-ego" response. It's more reflective and considered.

We want to look at the first, or id, response for a moment. It's very much like the reaction of the first, least experienced martial arts student. Let's briefly explore what some of the id responses look like, what might motivate them, and how to address them.

Often the first thing that a person feels when confronted with truth from another is *shock.* Quite often, anger follows the shock. When we hear a truth about ourselves from someone else, we may want to lash out, to hit back, to offer a payback for the pain we feel. The intensity of the anger can range from mild annoyance to rage. Like shock, this anger may pass quickly—or it can be prolonged.

Unless it's an extreme case, one of the best ways to deal with another person's shock is to allow some time to pass. Anger, on the other hand, can be quite intense and even frightening. It may require a more immediate solution. Therefore, unless you think someone reacting this way is prone to violence or might do harm to you or to himself, it often helps the person to let him vent. Understand this: An internal friction between the other person's reality and what you have just shared with him drives the anger. And friction creates heat. If you have lots of heat and no vent available for the heat to escape, the result could be worse than the heat of the moment. (We'll discuss that shortly.)

If you're the listener during the "anger ventilation" of someone else, it's crucial that you not allow yourself to respond in kind. Allow the person to vent her emotion, recognizing that it's coming out with less processing than normal. It's unvarnished and mixed up with a lot of other things. She may say things about you that are hurtful, shameful, and utterly despicable. But remember: *You are telling the truth only after you feel you have some grasp of the truth about your own shortcomings.*

Accept what you can and allow the rest to flow past you without a response. And be prepared to forgive what is said and move on into the restorative process.

As we said earlier, when someone has this anger well up within heart and mind, it creates heat. And if there isn't a place and time for that energy to go, it gets contained and can begin an emotional meltdown. Anger, whether directed by a person at himself or aimed at another without the ability for it to be aired, can create depression. Depression has mild and severe forms. The point is, allowing the articulation of the anger (or some inarticulate screams, or actions in more severe situations) can be disturbing and sometimes scary. Yet it's really a healthy part of the process you have started.

The apostle Paul, one of the writers of the New Testament, anticipated anger as a possible response to truth—and he understood the value of getting over that anger. Consider this piece of advice he offered to the early Christians in Ephesus:

> Therefore each of you must put off falsehood and speak truthfully to his neighbor, for we are all members of one body. "In your anger do not sin": Do not let the sun go down while you are still angry, and do not give the devil a foothold. (Ephesians 4:25-27)

As he is coming out of shock, a person who has heard some "tough truth" may just deny that anything has happened. He'll claim that he's "just fine, thank you." There's no display of emotion; it would appear that what has transpired has had no effect on him at all.

Just remember that appearances can be deceiving. What could actually be happening is that the shock has taken on a different form. The information is too overwhelming for him to handle. In response, the mind effectively seals everything up in some mental compartment and keeps it from being recognized as truth, much less dealt with.

In the vast majority of cases, the emotional experience of both truth-tellers and truth-hearers in a one-on-one situation are covered in the categories of shock and anger—usually in their milder forms. These emotions can be painful to experience, first or second hand. Occasionally, they can even be disturbing. Regardless, don't second-guess yourself as a truth-teller or truth-hearer.

If you're telling the truth after you've applied the Rule of Truth, what you're actually witnessing will be the rebirth of an emotional leper. You'll see nerves, apparently long dead or numb, coming alive. And in spite of the heavy emotion of the moment, you truly are witnessing something of a miracle.

If you're the hearer in this situation, keep in mind that you are the primary beneficiary of the miracle—and not a victim of cruelty.

If you long for this kind of miracle in you and those around you, you're not alone. Truth-telling and hearing are crucial to everyday integrity. Some three-quarters of those surveyed in a poll said that it was very desirable for them to be known as a person of integrity.[2]

There are others besides you for whom truth and integrity matter.

Responses to Truth Encounters: Thinking Carefully

After truth-telling causes an emotional response, there comes a more reflective (well, at least we hope so) response. In simple terms, there are fundamentally three of these more thoughtful responses to truth. Briefly stated, these are:

1. *I hear you and reject the truth of what you say.*

2. *I hear you and I believe the truth of what you say. But I refuse to do anything about it.*

3. *I hear you and I believe the truth of what you say. And I'm going to work with this truth in my life.*

When you're a truth-teller, you'll experience each of these responses at some point. You should be emotionally prepared to deal with each one, as difficult as it might be to accept.

First, there will be times when you confront people with the truth and they'll simply reject what you're saying to them. As youth pastors, both of us had truth-telling sessions — uncomfortable ones at that — with parents of the youth in our respective churches.

One Saturday morning, a mother of one of the youth — we'll call her Mrs. Ferguson — asked Steve to make the forty-five-minute drive from seminary to the church youth room. Once he arrived, he was greeted by a flood of tears. The mother composed herself after a few minutes, then began the discussion.

"It's come to my attention that Shelley is sleeping around."

Shelley was a fourteen-year-old eighth-grader at the time. Steve was as shocked to hear the news as Shelley's mother must have been. He went through the shock and anger — the id responses described earlier. Then they discussed family dynamics and what might have launched Shelley into such behavior.

"Steve, I'm just at a loss to figure this out. All I can tell you is that I'm glad I put her on the Pill a year ago."

"Excuse me. Would you repeat that?"

"I put her on the Pill. . . . Well, you know how horribly embarrassing it would be for Shelley to end up pregnant, what with my husband's position in his company and our responsibilities here at the church."

"Mrs. Ferguson, did you ever think that putting Shelley on the Pill at the age of thirteen might send some kind of message to her?"

"Like what?"

"Like you don't trust her to wait until marriage, perhaps. Or maybe that you're giving her permission to be sexually active now."

"Oh, no, it *couldn't* be that. Something else must have happened."

"Did you ever talk this over with Shelley?"

"No. Not really. . . . But it isn't because she's on the Pill."

When someone won't embrace the truth — as Steve found out — you can repackage what you're saying, you can continue over time to speak the truth again and again, but fundamentally you cannot force anyone to accept what you believe the truth to be. We must be very open to the fact that what we honestly and compassionately believe to be the truth might be misled, misinformed, or just misunderstood.

The second, and perhaps the most difficult situation to deal with, is when you confront people with the truth and they accept what you're saying, but essentially they don't care. They know you are right. Yet they treat your care, your input, and your compassion like refuse on the street. Often belligerent and defiant, these people can be very difficult to deal with on an ongoing basis.

Devlin encountered one such individual some years ago. He heard about a friend with a problem on the job. He took time off from his own job to be with his friend one day at work.

The problem was obvious: Devlin's friend, Joe, was spending so much time on office politics that he wasn't fulfilling his job description. Joe was in a position that demanded a certain amount of report generation every day. But he spent so much time hanging around the water cooler, so many moments in other people's offices, so much energy figuring out who he could stab in the back to his benefit, that the reports weren't getting done.

Devlin was cautious in his approach that day. "So, Joe, when do you have to have your dailies done for your supervisor?"

"Supposedly at 3:00. But I never meet that deadline."

"Are the reports important?"

"Oh, yeah. They end up as weekly summaries, then quarterly reviews."

"But they're not as important to you as schmoozing around the office, are they?"

"No. Not at all. I play this game to the hilt. Figure that'll do me more good than pushing paper."

"You're sure about that? Seems to me that you're in a pretty pivotal position, and that the company's counting on you for your analysis and reporting ability—not for your latest joke around the water cooler. You came to me to see if I could offer some perspective here. I think this is it: you should spend more time on the reports, and less time on the politics."

Joe sighed. "Aw, maybe you're right. But I've gone too far down this road to reverse gears now. I'll make it or break it on the politics. Thanks anyway."

The pink slip came to Joe's desk a week later. He heard the truth, believed the truth—and just didn't care enough about it to change his behavior.

But there is a third category of response to the truth. A response in this category will offer you the truth-telling experience that you hoped for from the beginning: Someone hears you and is willing to work with the truth you offer. This person helps herself to become more healthy, to behave in more-appropriate ways, or to relate to others better.

A friend of ours named Julie was seventeen when she lost her mother to cancer. There's no good time for such a loss, but it was particularly bitter for Julie as she was finishing high school and selecting a college.

Julie had three younger siblings. She had become a mother for them, and she kept that role as she stayed around her home town after graduating from high school. Julie decided to pursue an associate's degree at the local community college before moving on to the state university.

Almost three years after his wife's death, Julie's father fell in love with a young widow in town. They enjoyed a respectable relationship, but Julie's resentment toward her father's new love interest was almost tangible. She went to her mother's sister to talk about her feelings.

"Aunt Jane, I can't believe Dad's doing this!"

"It shows. But Julie, did you expect your father to wait until he was retirement age to find someone else?"

"And I can't believe you're so laid back about this! Mom was your sister, after all!"

"I know that. And I'll be the first to say it hurt at first to see your dad with Rita. But I know he still misses your mother. And I also know he wants to be a husband again and to have a mom in the house for your sister and brothers."

"But he has me!"

"Only until the fall. Then you're off for another degree. Julie, let me tell you what I figured out. You should think about applying this, too. I figured that we don't have to let anyone else take your mother's place in our hearts. But I believe we should make the extra room for Rita. Otherwise, we'll needlessly hurt some people we love. What do you say?"

It took some time, but Julie faced the truth about her situation and the need to let her father move on. When she did that, she was able to move on, too. She and Rita have been good friends for nearly a quarter-century now.

Reflecting on Our Responses

So what should you take away from this discussion about responses to truth? There are two reasons for talking about how people respond to the truth.

First, people who have a renewed enthusiasm for truth-telling are often under the misguided notion that once they start telling the truth, things will get better, everything will begin to work out, and the entire process will go more smoothly. The reality is that things become *healthier.* But there can and will be plenty of bumps in the road. One helpful perspective is to look at your truth-telling as being neutral. How another person chooses to respond is what creates the difficulties and potholes that make this process the ride of our lives.

The second reason is that as truth-tellers, it's important that we know and understand these responses, because we'll be given plenty of opportunities to experience them. Even if you begin to be a truth-teller for all the right reasons, your motives are pure, and you abide by the Rule of Truth, you'll find people who will tell you the truth about yourself only with a sense of vindictiveness and retribution. And if you know the possible responses to truth, you'll have a greater power to exercise self-discipline, graciousness, and love in response.

One last thing: reality is never that clean. We'd be amazed if you found a situation that fit exactly into the paradigms we have discussed. Instead, the situations you encounter will blend together in an infinite number of forms. But if you can think through the truth-telling situation and boil it down to basics, it will become apparent which of the three responses to the truth is operative at the moment.

truth in the family truth in the family truth in the family truth in the family truth in the family truth in the family in the family truth in the family truth in the family truth in the family truth in the family truth in the family truth truth in the family truth in the family truth in the

Chapter

6 ▶ truth in the family

The greatest homage we can pay to truth is to use it.
—Ralph Waldo Emerson

There's a legend from the Old West about some thieves who came upon a safe that had fallen from the back of an army buckboard.

That safe held two months' payroll for the soldiers in four forts. It was a fortune waiting to be spent—if the thieves could only get to it. But these particular bandits weren't very sophisticated. They'd only dealt in the realm of "stick 'em up" stagecoach heists and the occasional bank robbery. They'd never had to break into a safe before.

First they tried shooting a hole in the safe. They aimed their pistols and a rifle or two at the same place on the side of the safe. A few dozen bullets barely scratched the safe's surface. So they took iron bars and sticks to the area around the combination lock. This effort nicked the lock's paint, but not much more.

They decided to wander into the realm of explosives. They placed three sticks of dynamite under the safe and lit them. They blew a nice-sized hole in the ground under the safe, but barely moved—much less damaged—the safe itself.

The hapless thieves were getting frustrated. They decided to load the safe back onto a buckboard. They took it to the edge of a two-hundred-foot cliff. Surely the fall to the rocks below would break something loose, right?

They watched in hope as the safe tumbled down the cliff, with a couple of dramatic bounces off the cliff wall. There was a large *boom* as it hit the canyon floor. The thieves made their way down a switchback road that led to the site of the fall.

When they got there, the safe was dusty—but hardly damaged.

Finally, they decided to let the army know where the safe was. At least then they could collect the reward money. They made the contact at the nearest fort. Claiming they had found the safe on the way through the gully while they were hunting rabbits, they led the troops to it.

The thieves watched in even greater frustration as some corporal—barely old enough to shave—pulled a piece of paper from his pocket and turned the combination lock tumblers this way, then that way, then back again. With a twist of the handle, the corporal opened the safe door.

And there it was—gold to back up the army payroll for thousands of troops.

To their credit, the thieves never had a second thought about trying to overpower the army personnel. With the soldiers outnumbering them at a nearly twenty-to-one ratio, it didn't seem like such a good idea.

Instead, they waited as the captain in charge of the mission stepped forward and took two gold ingots from the safe. He even saluted them as he handed the ingots to one of the thieves. Then the troops loaded the safe onto their army buckboard. The thieves watched as they disappeared into a cloud of dust.

Jesse, the leader of the desperadoes, clanked the two ingots together thoughtfully. "That kid just . . . just *opened* that safe! After all we went through, to think that some peach-fuzz-lipped kid opened the safe!"

Jared, his brother, sidled up beside Jesse and shrugged. "We could have saved a lot of time, too, if we just had the combination."

There's a moral to this story: If you want to get to the gold, you need to use the right combination. In the same way, if you want to get to the treasure that is the truth, you need to apply the right combination of action.

That's why we're turning our discussion of truth toward ways you can "get to the gold" of truth in your family, in your workplace, and in our society. We won't be talking about the theory of truth—we'll be talking about using the truth.

To this point, we have made our case for the importance of truth in a very general way. We used multiple illustrations as we were going, but now we've reached a point where we want to take all of this abstract knowledge and begin to apply it in very specific ways.

And the best place to start, as far as we can tell, is right at home.

The Joy of an Honest Home

We first want to look at the role of truth in the family. Why? Because of the Danish philosopher Søren Kierkegaard. He pointed out that the exploration and practice of truth requires a certain degree of vulnerability:

> In order to swim one takes off all one's clothes—in order to aspire to the truth one must undress in a far more inward sense, divest oneself of all one's inward clothes, of thoughts, conceptions, selfishness etc. before one is sufficiently naked.[1]

Nowhere else are we as vulnerable—in relationships that demand trust—as in the family. The same kind of comfort that produces the ability to walk around the home in less-than-public dress can be the perfect atmosphere to encourage truth-telling, truth-hearing—and the benefits of both.

You may rightly argue that truth has disappeared from a number of environments in our society. We maintain that this is simply a result of truth doing a disappearing act in too many of our families. We tend to agree with those who position the family as the building block of our society. We fundamentally believe that the family is the unit that provides training that either builds character in a methodical and intentional way or leaves the character of a child to develop subject to the whims of current culture or thought.

The Bond of Marriage

The family can be defined in many ways. It has been examined at different places in its development. At the risk of acting arbitrarily, we'll start our discussion of truth in the family with marriage.

We define marriage as the commitment of a man and a woman, one to another. Traditionally, these individuals make vows to each other. Since the social revolution and experimentation of the 1960s, these vows have come under no small amount of discussion, derision, and in many cases, rejection.

We believe that it's crucial for a couple to commit—before their vows are even spoken—that in their relationship they'll be ruthlessly honest, employing the principle that we've already discussed at length: the Rule of Truth. Both husband and wife need to be honest with themselves about their own strengths and weaknesses and to address the strengths and weaknesses of their mates with the same honesty and the same careful tenderness that they bring to their own self-evaluation.

This is nothing new in successful marriages, of course. Steve's maternal grandparents, Roy and Nell, enjoyed six decades of marriage keeping that principle alive in their relationship. It saw them through hard years on the farm, the Great Depression, starts on a variety of careers, and a lot of life.

It also saw them through a delicate negotiation that has destroyed other families. Roy was an alcoholic. For years, he was a "functioning drinker"—in fact, he enjoyed success on the job and respect as a hard worker. But thirty years into their marriage, after the children were grown, after they had moved to the homestead where they hoped to retire, Roy began to black out. He became more irrational when he was drunk. He was getting mean.

It took a lot of courage in those days for a wife to confront a husband. But Nell prefaced her confrontation with "Now, Roy, you know we promised to be honest with each other. And now it's time to talk about your drinking." And Roy couldn't argue with their commitment to be honest with each other. In fact, he suddenly became aware of how *dishonest* he had become in their relationship by trying to cover up his drinking problem for so many years. He began his trek back to sobriety that day, a move that almost certainly saved their marriage—and his life.

Doesn't a commitment to openness and honesty make sense in a marriage? Sadly, a commitment to honesty is neither obvious nor put into practice in many relationships. Rather than taking the time to discuss areas of friction or conflict, many people choose short-term peace over long-term health. And that, as we have discussed, leads to a numbing of our emotional nerves, which is the beginning of what we earlier called "emotional leprosy."

Once emotional leprosy affects a marriage, two things will likely happen. First, it probably will take a major jolt to jumpstart the emotional system again. Little hits along the way, although painful, will be encountered, absorbed, and processed. And the partners will move on. If it takes a significant jolt to bring their feelings back to life, the unfortunate result is pain in a concentrated and compounded form.

Our friend Barry had such a wake-up call fifteen years into his marriage. He was putting in too much time at the office. His wife, Sue, felt she was carrying too much of the burden at home. One Wednesday evening, after another day of too many hours at work, Barry came home to find Sue throwing some clothes into a suitcase.

"I can't take it anymore," Sue said, refusing to let her eyes meet Barry's as she packed. "You're never here. You don't make it to the kids' soccer games. We're behind on the bills, you need a raise, and I don't believe all the time you put into the company is getting us ahead at all. I need a break. I'm out of here."

The news hit Barry with a crushing force. He knew Sue was right. He also knew that if he let her leave without acknowledging her feelings, she might not come back.

"Wait a minute. Can you put this off for one week? Tell me the things you want me to change right now. If I don't make them happen in the next seven days, I'll buy you a ticket to wherever you want to go."

That offer let Sue know that Barry was taking her seriously—a pleasant surprise in itself. She finally looked Barry in the eyes and said, "You're on. First, Jerry has a game Friday afternoon at 4:00 at Pioneer Park. Be there. Second, tomorrow morning before you leave I want you to talk to all three of the kids. Just acknowledge that they exist before they go to school, okay? Third, how about leaving the office at 5:00 every night for the next week just to let me know that you're capable of it?"

The force of Sue's words continued to settle on Barry. He had no argument. There would be assignments to postpone and appointments to reschedule—and everything in him let him know Sue was at the end of her patience. "Fair enough."

Sue then began to unpack her suitcase.

Barry told us later that he went directly from that encounter into the bathroom, where he first threw up and then started to cry. It was a shock to his system. He'd been blindsided by the confrontation. But that was the beginning of his recovery from emotional leprosy in his marriage.

The second thing that usually happens when emotional leprosy visits a marriage is that one or both partners begin to receive emotional wounds. These wounds may be small, and often are unintentional. But due to the numbness from the couple's lack of feeling, they don't even recognize this small damage. They don't address the wound, clean it up, or work to heal it. And the open wound begins to show signs of infection. The infection grows and begins to affect their emotional health, and they're still unaware.

This is what many people are referring to when they talk about "baggage" in a relationship. Baggage is the emotional scars and infections that cause someone to act or react in a certain fashion that is unintentional, yet nearly inevitable.

Lynne had been overweight—not grossly so—for most of her marriage to Lee. Lee was mildly bothered by Lynne's weight now and then, but not enough to make an issue of it. Lynne was far more sensitive about her weight than he was, and it just didn't seem to be a worthwhile subject to keep in the limelight of their marriage. Lynne and Lee seemed to reach a silent agreement that the subject of Lynne's weight would not be a topic of discussion.

We're not about to suggest anything subliminal was happening, but an unusual phenomenon emerged in their home after this tacit agreement was reached: Lee began singing the chorus to "Too Fat Polka" while he was tinkering around the house. You know—the one with the line, "She's too fat for me."

For months, Lynne didn't realize the hit she was taking every time she heard those words come out of Lee's mouth. And understand, Lee didn't intend them to wound Lynne. He thought he was just singing an old song. At first Lynne thought so, too. But over time, her feelings grew from mild irritation to near rage when she heard Lee launch into the chorus. Every time she heard the words, she was reminded of her weight problem. She felt more helpless than ever to do anything about it—and she began to wonder if Lee meant what he was singing.

Finally, Lynne couldn't take it anymore. While Lee was replacing the trim around their bedroom door one day, singing his usual offering as he worked, Lynne confronted him with some heat in her voice. "Don't you know any other songs?"

"What? I guess so. What's wrong with this one?"

"Just think about what you're singing. *Do you mean it?*"

"Mean *what?*"

"That I'm too fat for you. You used to talk to me about that, you know."

Lee was dumbstruck. "Okay, honey. Then I won't sing it anymore."

"That's not good enough. We need to talk about this. I feel really bad about my weight. I think it bothers you, too. And I need to know if we need to do something about it."

So they talked. They spoke and heard the truth from each other. Lynne told Lee about her constant worry that she wasn't attractive to him anymore. Lee told Lynne about his concern that she didn't feel good about herself, and how he felt that he needed to walk on eggshells now and then to make sure he didn't offend her with some offhand comment.

The beauty of the situation? You're probably expecting that Lynne went on a catabolic diet, lost twenty pounds, and they lived happily ever after. Not so. Lynne and Lee determined together that Lynne's weight wasn't a threat to her health. Lee assured Lynne that it wasn't a threat to his desire for her, either. They caught an issue that was causing little wounds between them before it festered into something bigger.

And, for whatever reason, Lee now sings "Smoke on the Water" while he works around the house. We have no idea why.

Marriage is about sharing and helping each other become healthier, more complete people. We share the pains and the joys. And it's the pain that brings the real payoff when we feel joy. Rather than run from ourselves, the truth allows us to embrace who we are — just as we are — and grow from it.

That was the gift Lynne and Lee gave each other by truth-telling and truth-hearing in their marriage. Truth-telling is fundamental to this process of building a healthy marriage. You can't find a healthy marriage without a liberal application of the Rule of Truth, a healthy mixture of honest feelings, and prompt attention to the little emotional cuts and scrapes that we absorb along the way.

The long and the short of it is this: *Healthy people feel pain when something is wrong.* Pain serves a vital purpose in our lives, and we need it. Not telling (or hearing) the truth only makes us less healthy and creates a fear of pain, the one thing that will help us become better people — and better spouses.

The Development of Children

Children often provide some of a couple's greatest joys. Paradoxically, children are also perhaps the biggest responsibility anyone encounters.

Among the responsibilities we assume with children is a duty to teach them how to survive in a world where things often go awry. And the goal is not just to survive, but to survive in as healthy a way as possible. That includes learning how to apply the Rule of Truth.

Learning to apply the Rule of Truth has immediate benefits for children and those around them. Yet there's also a long-range purpose for teaching children that rule: to give them a foundation for their future roles in their marriages, in their families, in their work, and in society in general. One of the foundational issues for healthy relationships of any kind is the ability to trust. And as we covered earlier, truth-telling is an essential and indispensable element for trust to develop.

Whether or not we like to admit it, whether we accept or reject the notion, our children look to us, individually and specifically, to learn how to navigate life. We may believe strongly that there are many other influences in life beyond the parent — and certainly there are — yet given the amount of time parents spend with their children and their proximity to them, the ability to have a major impact on a child is dramatic.

And that impact happens not just during the times when we willingly, knowingly tell untruth, bend the truth, or work around the truth—with the intent of doing damage. It also happens when we are being positive, encouraging, and supportive of our children. We all love to think that each child—especially our own—is capable of doing whatever he or she desires. The thinking goes, "With enough hard work, enough effort and support and opportunity provided by us, their parents, there's nothing our children cannot do."

This is where the Rule of Truth *must* begin to affect how we deal with our children. And because what we're about to discuss might be misapplied, it's with great care that we broach this particular point.

Make no mistake: encouragement, love, and unconditional acceptance are required to raise healthy children. But so is the acceptance of the fact that God made each one of us individually. And if we are unique individuals, then each of us cannot be capable of accomplishing anything and everything by sheer force of will. That would, in fact, make us all the same: identical except in the strength and purity of our will, our ability to harness and channel our desires.

Rafe and Gisele Martin were both professional musicians before they married. Everyone—including Rafe and Gisele—assumed that their offspring would be musical prodigies.

Two of their children, Cynthia and Rey, were just that. If it had to do with music, they could do it, and do it well. They both had perfect pitch. They performed with a maturity beyond their years. When they joined with Rafe and Gisele to perform, it was a joy to hear.

Another child, Jack, showed no promise as a performer whatsoever. Yet Rafe and Gisele believed it to be only a matter of time until Jack blossomed musically. They thought they just needed to help him discover that gift. So Jack was forced into piano lessons, then trumpet lessons, then voice lessons at home. But in every musical endeavor, he just couldn't keep up with his siblings.

As a result, by the age of eight Jack felt he was a failure. He felt like an outcast in his own family. The truth of the matter was, he couldn't perform to his family's musical standards—and from all indications never would. Yet he bravely kept going to lesson after lesson.

A kind guitar instructor named Bernie walked into his home studio one day to see Jack standing at the studio window, watching the activity in the backyard. Bernie's sons were in back playing soccer.

"Hey, Jack. Do you like to play soccer?"

"I've only tried it on the playground a couple of times. Mom and Dad aren't much for sports."

"Really? Tell you what. Why don't you go kick the ball around with the boys for a few minutes while I tune our guitars?"

"Really?"

"Go for it. I'll call you in when I'm finished."

Tuning the guitars was a two-minute task at most for Bernie. But Jack had struggled so much during the lessons that Bernie felt sorry for him. Bernie watched as Jack made his way into the pickup game the boys were enjoying—and he saw Jack transform.

The insecure child musician was having his way with Bernie's sons as they kicked the ball around. Jack had a natural rhythm with a soccer ball that Bernie had never seen him have with a guitar. He flowed with the ball's movement back and forth across the yard. He stole the ball from Bernie's sons with ease. He seemed to be able to kick the ball wherever he wanted to.

Rafe was surprised at Bernie's request later that day: "I'll give you the next ten lessons—no charge—if you let Jack play soccer with my sons this season."

It was an unusual request, but Rafe thought the exercise would do Jack some good. He agreed.

Jack blossomed on the soccer field; his lessons with Bernie didn't bear much fruit. By the end of the season, Rafe and Gisele accepted the fact that Jack's gifts simply lay somewhere else than the arena of musical performance.

At this writing, Cynthia and Rey are both in college on music scholarships. They're destined for big things. Jack, having played varsity soccer since his freshman year, is about to graduate from high school. He's looking at scholarship offers from a dozen different major universities interested in his soccer skills. He's well adjusted and jokes about being the family's only nonmusician.

Do we advocate starting at birth offering harsh insights into a child's abilities and weaknesses directly to the child? Absolutely not. On the other hand, we don't advocate parents pushing their children to excel at something for which they have little or no aptitude. In those cases, parents need to tell themselves the truth and then help their children find their own God-given gifts and talents.

Parents also need to give positive, clear, and consistent encouragement so their children will use their strengths well. But it's just as positive for children to know that there will be some things that will always challenge them, just as there are other things they can excel at.

We also need to communicate clearly when talking with our children. We may be proud of them. We may be thrilled at what they're able to accomplish as they excel in their strengths and overcome their weaknesses. However, we need to examine our use of superlatives when talking with our children about their gifts and abilities.

We should always talk about a child's intrinsic value and personal worth in the most glowing terms. But talk surrounding a child's behaviors, gifts, and abilities—while addressed in caring and loving terms—should be based firmly in reality. The more accurate and complete an idea children have of who they are and what they can do, the more confident they become. Living under the illusion that they'll always succeed can, in fact, set them up to fail. And the unexpected failure could inhibit them and erode their confidence. Unrealistic expectations from overenthusiastic parents can hinder children from engaging life fully.

Truth Is a Two-Way Street

All parents will, at some level, work with their children to help them understand that they must tell the truth when dealing with others. This process begins early and seems never-ending for parents. The earliest and most frequent application usually involves calling children to account for their behavior.

"Josh, who broke the lamp?"

Josh is in the living room. The end of his baseball bat is sticking out from beneath the sofa. He's nearly in tears before he answers.

At such a moment, parents clearly don't want to sift through layers of stories to find out what happened. They want the child to tell them exactly what happened with no embellishment. The parents want to be able to trust what the child is saying to them. Fair enough. But do parents demonstrate the same type of commitment to truthful behavior in their own lives—lives lived in full view of their child?

Parents have multiple opportunities each day to demonstrate how important it is to live a truthful life. The phone rings. Someone answers and announces to the family that the phone is for Dad. Dad is tired from a long day's work. Should he respond, "Just tell them I'm not here" and expect Josh to 'fess up about the lamp?

Mom is at the grocery store. She receives change for her purchase—five dollars too much. She counts her money outside the store and recognizes the mistake. Does she take the money back to the cashier? Does she hide the money quickly inside her purse? Is her position that truth matters when it doesn't cost her anything, but when it pays to hide the truth she should feel free to conceal reality?

Sure, these are little things. But it's the little things that build upon each other and ultimately create what becomes character. We jeopardize the character of our children when we don't properly focus on the important issues of truth.

Building character is no different from building anything else. Every piece that goes higher builds on what came before. If what came before is inconsistent, things get off track. Character goes awry.

This is the opposite of what we discussed in chapter 1 when tackling the concept of the ethics of exception. The ethics of exception is when we try to build a moral position for everyday conduct from some extreme and usually rare occurrence. What we're talking about with our children is building the ethics of the everyday. It's not the fringe situation that will deeply affect our children and move them off the moral center we are working hard to build into them. It's the exceptions we regularly and consistently allow to the standard of truth and integrity in everyday life. It's the regular and consistent exceptions to truthful conduct that we make daily—offering no explanation or demonstrating no consistency in our behavior—that will begin to warp the character of our children.

How does it warp them? We demonstrate that there are no consequences to untruthful behavior or speech. We act as if the avoidance of discomfort or pain by bending the truth is a perfectly acceptable behavior. And with each occurrence, we run the risk that it's *this* time that we begin to inhibit the character development of our children.

One final note: your children are built to trust your promises.

We both travel extensively, and for a time we both traveled internationally. When Steve's children were younger, he'd make a cassette tape of lullabies and stories for them to listen to while he was gone. (They made a tape for Steve to listen to, as well. Make a note: great idea for dads traveling away from their families.)

After one very draining journey to Africa, Steve got off the plane and said to his children, "Wow, will it feel good to tuck you both in 'live and in person' tonight."

His daughter, Maggie, asked, "Will you sing to us?"

His son, Ben, chimed in, "Daddy, you'll tell us a story from Africa tonight, won't you?"

"I promise."

But the hours before bedtime proved longer than Steve expected. He was exhausted by bedtime, and he tried to beg off the lullabies and story. Ben and

Maggie were understandably disappointed. Steve suggested a compromise: "Hey, you could listen to Daddy's tape one more night."

Ben shook his head. "But the tape doesn't rock us in the rocking chair."

Maggie looked at her brother and nodded. "And you promised."

Steve and his kids fell asleep in the rocking chair midway through the giraffe story that night. Since then, he has been both haunted and encouraged by the weight children give to their parents' promises.

At home—maybe more than in any other environment—it's apparent that the "little everyday ways" we handle truth and truth-telling behaviors have a far greater effect than the arguments that rage about the exceptions. Here, in the grist of everyday life, the elements of character and truth-telling come together to build a child's ability to trust others.

If we don't build this ability to have some acceptable range of trust in others, then truth in the workplace and truth in society (the subjects of the next two chapters) become problematic. The basic building blocks of truth-telling must be in place in the home environment. Children and parents must establish trust if they are to act with character and integrity when engaging situations beyond their own immediate family.

The home should be a haven for every child. Children should be loved, accepted, and cared for at every turn. But truthful input from parents, both in word and in deed, is critical for children to gain a good, strong, and clear sense of who they are and what their gifts are.

This means that we parents must apply the Rule of Truth at least as much in dealing with children as in dealing with adults. But the payoff is well worth it: children will develop an unbreakable trust with their parents when they know that they can count on what their parents say.

truth in the workplace truth in the workplace truth in the workplace truth in the workplace truth in the workplace truth in the workplace truth in the workplace truth in the workplace truth in the workplace truth in the workplace truth in the workplace truth in the workplace truth in the workplace truth in the workplace truth in the work

Chapter 7 ▶ truth in the workplace

> In this life of illusion and quasi-illusion, the person of solid virtues who can be admired for something more substantial than his well-knownness often proves to be the unsung hero: the teacher, the nurse, the mother, the honest cop, the hard worker at lonely, underpaid, unglamorous, unpublicized jobs.
> —Daniel J. Boorstin

John worked for a closely held, family-owned company. The Midwestern values that built the company permeated its corporate ethos. Larger companies might overlook behavior issues in middle management that John knew would never fly in small-town, midstate Illinois.

John was a sales manager in a highly competitive industry. He reformed an unmotivated regional sales force into a dynamo. It was a three-year process, but in his region, his team dominated industry sales.

To mark four quarters at the top of their region, John decided to host a celebration for his team. His complete sales staff and Marty, the company's vice president for marketing and sales, were there. Caught up in the revelry of the event,

John had too much to drink. He caused no overt embarrassment to anyone. He simply asked that someone drive him home.

John was fully sober and able to come to work the next morning. He actively participated in a three-hour meeting with his sales staff and Marty. It was a lively discussion, full of optimism and promise. There were minor points of disagreement between John and some of his staff, and between John and Marty. John thought the points of dissension were just part of the process and that everybody had the opportunity to contribute.

His sales staff walked out the door on the way to lunch. Each of them, including those who had disagreed with John at some time during the meeting, shook hands with him and thanked him for a productive morning.

Marty had a different read on the situation. After the last salesperson had left, he shut the door to the conference room and faced John. "John, I want you to know I've come to a decision. Based on last night, and what I saw here this morning, I'll have to mention in my record of this meeting that you were drunk last night."

"You'll have to *what?* What was wrong with this morning?"

"You just didn't seem to make sense to me."

"Just because we didn't agree on a few points, you think I'm coming to work loaded?"

Marty just shrugged and walked out of the room.

John felt the knot form and twist in his gut. He knew that Marty's own position was in jeopardy. Marty was famous, in fact, for writing reports questioning the judgment and behavior of those who worked for him. He seemed threatened by anyone who showed initiative. John had not yet been on the receiving end of that poison pen. But he had a feeling he was about to know what it was like.

Later that afternoon, John was summoned to Marty's office. "I think you should know what I put in my write-up of this morning's meeting, John." The hard copy of the report was on the desk. The final bullet point read, "Content of the meeting may have been influenced by John's drinking."

John shook his head, but stayed surprisingly calm. "You know, that insinuates that alcohol influences me on the job. That's never been the case. It wasn't this morning. I didn't even have a hangover today. I've never come to work with one. But if you leave this point in, you could cost me my job."

"I'm sorry, John. That's the way I see it. That's what will go on record."

"Well, then, I guess I'll have to offer a similar observation about you. Remember, I have to report on this morning's meeting, too." John picked up a marker and wrote on Marty's white board, "Marty was sober today." Then he looked over to Marty, who was already turning red from the collar up.

"What are you trying to pull off?" Marty was whispering through his rage. "Anyone who reads that could think that the norm is for me to come to work drunk!"

"A half-truth meets a half-truth, Marty. What's your pleasure?"

Truth on the Job

We wish we could tell you that Marty and John ended the day in a big hug singing camp choruses around the water cooler. But they didn't.

Instead, they each included their half-truths in their meeting reports. They were both called in to explain their reports. The standoff made it clear that these two weren't going to be able to work together, so despite John's success and Marty's seniority, they were both asked for their resignations.

We can't say what would have happened had they both chosen to operate as fully in truth as possible. John could have left out the dig at Marty; Marty could have expressed disagreement with John's thinking without suggesting a problem with sobriety.

Maybe we're all just caught up in the culture. As much as we say we value truth and integrity as a society, we're still split on the application of that truth. A recent survey showed that one-third of us believe that there are unchanging moral absolutes, one-third believe that moral truth is relative to the circumstances, and one-third hold no position on moral truth or have never really thought about it.[1]

Do you really know how your coworkers are going to respond to truth in the workplace? For that matter, do you know how *you'll* respond?

There are places in each of our lives where truthfulness seems to be a more obvious choice than in others. As a culture that reveres the workplace, the vast majority of people will—at least at face value—affirm the need for honesty and personal integrity at work. But from the factory floor to the computer-chip clean room to the boardroom, there are less-obvious applications of truth. At least, that is, until we apply the Rule of Truth.

Positive Feedback

In this book, telling the truth is often equated with having to tell someone something difficult. But the fact of the matter is—and this is true in the family, at work, and in society—*learning how to give someone positive feedback about what they are doing can be at least as difficult as learning how to give input about negative or destructive behaviors.* In our society, we almost expect people to ignore the difficult things. But we all deeply desire for people to see us—really see us—as we do something well.

Katie was a gifted graphic designer. She worked hard at her craft for years and succeeded in establishing a successful part-time design business out of her home. When her youngest child reached second grade, Katie and her husband decided she could become a full-time employee again.

It seemed the time was right for that decision. One of Katie's clients was a catalog publisher who consistently raved about her work. The publisher courted Katie to come on board as staff. The deal was struck, and Katie was in without having to even look at another option.

Less than a month later, it seemed that Katie couldn't do anything right. She knew she was doing the same quality of work she'd done as a contractor, but all the publisher told her about were her mistakes. Katie simply wasn't receiving any positive feedback.

Six months later, Katie resigned her position. It was a complete surprise to the publisher, who took it upon himself to conduct the exit interview.

"Katie, what happened? I loved your work. You were taking us to another level of excellence. Did someone else give you an offer I need to match?"

It was Katie's turn to be surprised. "You know, if you loved my work, it would have been nice to hear about it now and then."

The publisher thought about it for a moment. "Maybe you're right." Katie's decision to return to freelancing was firm, but the publisher made it a point from that day on to comment on the good things his workers were doing—and his employee turnover went down dramatically.

Suspiciously Positive Feedback

That being said, for any of us to offer praise or affirmation that is not based on truth is just as dishonoring, just as dishonest, as using truth as a weapon or ignoring things that need to be addressed. We all want to be affirmed for the things we do well or the improvements we're making. Yet too much uncritical praise makes us wonder about the truthfulness of the praise we're receiving.

Devlin is a regular commentator on popular culture. Recently he was reading a book by Joe Jackson, a pop musician who reached his zenith in the early eighties.

What's fascinating for many Americans to discover is that many pop musicians like Jackson have serious musical training. Jackson himself studied at the Royal Academy of Music in London. In his autobiography, *A Cure for Gravity*, Jackson relates his experience of "suspiciously positive feedback" from a percussion instructor:

> He was very old, and the most encouraging teacher I have ever come across. He would stop me and exclaim "Oh very good!" after practically each hit of a drum or tap of a tambourine. He was so encouraging, in fact, that I started to wonder if he was senile. For all his vast experience, I learned very little from him.[2]

It felt good for Jackson to receive the praise from his percussion instructor. But the praise was so frequent, and so often it seemed for nothing, that after some time Jackson began to doubt the veracity of anything his instructor said.

The lesson here is simple: when offering positive observations about a person's behavior, it's important to be as specific and detail-oriented as we are when pointing out negative issues. Even praise has to be based in reality. Remember that the Rule of Truth doesn't apply solely to difficult situations. It also applies to those times when we're affirming people.

We talked in chapter 1 about our friend Bill who went through his work life thinking that his performance on the job was at least acceptable, if not downright outstanding. Then came the fateful day when his boss had to let him know that his work wasn't at a level where the company could afford to keep him on—or even work with him for improvement.

The question that we ask you to consider now is this: who was at fault in this situation? To some of this misled gentleman's coworkers, the man himself was obviously at fault. His work habits and ability to perform the job were clearly less than the minimum standard they expected from someone at the company. Certainly, a large part of the blame does lie with the worker himself.

But we believe that this explanation is too easy. Blaming the person, while perhaps legitimate at some level, isn't the solution to this more complex equation. The answer, like the problem, has more to it:

- ▶ Had this worker heard about his performance deficiencies on a regular basis?

- ▶ Had someone invested the time and energy to let him see himself as the others working in his area saw him?

- ▶ Had anyone cared enough about him to share the truth of his substandard work performance, just as that person would have wished someone had talked to him if the shoe happened to be on the other foot?

These are important questions for all of us, whether leaders or followers, in a company or organization. How can we be expected to correct anything about ourselves if we're not in a position to accurately see what kind of a worker we really are? And not the person we think we are, but the person others experience.

We both have served in supervisory positions in a large company. As consultants, we both have been asked to honestly evaluate the function of task forces, departments, and individuals alike.

Frankly, we're both pretty good at pointing out people's strengths. And we both look at encounters where corrective truth has to be stated as a bit like a trip to the dentist's chair—we know it's necessary, but it can be a white-knuckle event.

The biggest favor any supervisor did for either of us was to tell us about our blind spots. At one time or another in corporate cultures, we've both been informed about a need for a haircut or a different mode of dress. We both have heard about unintentional offenses to others. We corrected what we could in response to those sessions, and we were able to continue working well in those contexts.

In the same way, we feel the biggest favor we can do for others under our evaluation is to work with them on blind spots. Yet we take care to point out strengths as well as weaknesses. We challenge others, much as we were challenged, to take full advantage of their innate gifts and talents. We applaud their application and improvement of skills. That makes corrective truth easier to handle—and puts it into a reality-based context.

The challenge for a supervisor or manager is to be a true mirror for the people she serves. She's put in leadership positions to offer clear, constructive, and positive feedback about the performance—both exceptional and subpar—of those she supervises. But because of the many fears that surround truth-telling and truth-hearing, many managers actually look for ways to avoid talking honestly and clearly with those who work for them.

Sure, these discussions are difficult. Sometimes they get emotional. Sometimes there are tears, frustrations, and even conflict. But the positive payoff is huge, if often delayed. To see the workers you serve respond to clear feedback is both gratifying and humbling.

At this point, we could optimize our argument here by stating that if you tell others in your workplace the truth, everything will work out just fine. Of course, that's not always true. In fact, truth-telling on the job can be difficult and occasionally even heartbreaking. But remember, unless you give people a chance to see themselves in your feedback, they may never have the chance to change. To risk the truth is not always successful. Yet even if conflict comes with it, the truth is the best chance we have to help others.

That is, after all, the main point of workplace truth-telling: to help and to affirm.

A Winning Tactic: Turn the Truth on Yourself

One final issue here: How do we respond when things go wrong for us on the job? What do you do when you make a decision and it turns out to be wrong? What should you do when, in the course of business, your ability to control all the details is outstripped by reality? What happens when the results are not at all what you desired, what you worked for, or what you promised to others?

Brad faced that situation in a not-for-profit organization he served some years ago. He had built a team of young workers ready to take on the world. They had a cause that was gaining publicity and positive press. Brad had been told he was three months away from launching a new campaign, which would call for both the restructuring of his department and promotions for many of his protégés.

Brad was concerned about the time it would take to launch the new departmental structure. He decided to let his team members in on the upcoming change so that they could be prepared for their revised roles.

The problem was, that change never took place. The decision makers determined that such a shift in Brad's department was too much, too quickly. Brad was left to face his team.

He took the heat by taking the responsibility. "I made something sound certain that was still under discussion. In all honesty, *I* thought it was a done deal. But it wasn't. I know we've put a lot of effort and hope into what seems to be so much vapor right now. Please forgive me—but I wouldn't blame you if you didn't."

If anyone was thinking about leaving Brad's department in the heat of the moment, those thoughts were defused by that simple, straightforward statement. Brad communicated clearly about what had happened. He made no excuses. He put himself at his team's mercy.

So what would you have done? It's at this point of personal failure on the job that the Rule of Truth comes into play yet again. Sometimes we desire that those who work for us stand up and shoulder some of the responsibility for our mistakes—a kind of exercise in team loyalty. At other times, we find ourselves in a situation where we're in a desperate search for somewhere to deflect the responsibility or for an explanation that will take away our personal culpability.

At this point, we apply a strong, clear, and unwavering look at ourselves. Did we miscalculate? Did we err in our judgment? If so, then we need to stand and take responsibility for those actions.

This is where character comes into play. By accepting responsibility when it's genuinely ours, we exercise our ability to develop our character to a new level. Generally, rather than create more problems, we expand our self-esteem, we keep our self-respect, and we gain the respect of those around us.

None of this is to say that by owning up to your responsibility you will circumvent any consequences your actions have set in motion. But better to have the reputation as a person who does the right thing: taking responsibility for your actions. Living with the result of your actions, rather than manipulating the facts and the system to avoid any pain, is an honorable choice.

The work world takes up nearly a third of our lives. To disconnect the values that we learn and develop in our families from the world of our work can create significant frustration for us. Rather than passively sit by and allow ourselves to be compromised at work, we need to integrate our lives and our values.

the impact of truth the impact of truth the impact
of truth the impact of truth the impact of truth the
impact of truth the impact of truth the impact of
truth the impact of truth the impact of truth the
impact of truth the impact of truth the impact of
truth the impact of truth the impact of truth the
impact of truth the impact of truth the impact of

Chapter

8 ▶ truth in society

Every violation of truth is a stab at the health of human society.
—Ralph Waldo Emerson

We once heard the story of an aging count who loved to host costume balls. He delighted in studying the guests in their costumes. Instead of the tradition of having the guests unmask themselves an hour before the party's end, the count would line up the guests and guess who was behind each costume. As the years passed, the count's talent for guessing who was behind a mask reached near-perfection.

"Uncle, I don't see how you do it," the count's young grandnephew Jeremy remarked. Jeremy had come to visit so he could see his elder in action. "This guessing through the masks has earned you quite a reputation."

"Then it's time you learned something. Watch and listen carefully." The count led his young relative to an opera box in the estate's ballroom that allowed them a clear view of the guests. "Do you see the tiger over there? That's Williston. Fancies himself a predator in his business, so he comes dressed like one. Last time he was a jaguar. Obvious theme in his life.

"And that demure thing dressed like Little Bo Peep? Dame Jacqueline spent so much of her youth in wild living, she's been trying to recover her innocence ever since. She comes costumed like something innocent, because she wishes she were.

"Shakespeare down and to the left is Hobson. He writes advertising copy. Whines about no one appreciating his talent. He's always threatening to quit and write the novel of his generation. I wish he would. Last time he came as Dickens. Perhaps he should have repeated that costume; he really doesn't have the legs for tights.

"Cleopatra in the center of the room is Miss Wells. Looking for the Mark Antony to complete her kingdom. She'll always want to be a ruler, not a partner. Two parties ago, as I recall, she came as Catherine the Great. Not one to share her power."

Jeremy whistled through his teeth. "You're something, Uncle."

The count smiled. "All you need to know is that their real character is revealed by what they hide behind."

And that night, an hour before the party ended, the count guessed who was behind every mask.

Known by Our Masks

This fable was structured around a thought from Ralph Waldo Emerson. Emerson once compared society to a masked ball, where all could be known by their masks. He is still right. We put on the masks we think will hide our short-comings. Yet those very costumes reveal who we really are.

As a society, we tend to mask the effects of aging by dressing younger, driving a sports car, maybe even finding a younger "trophy" spouse to replace the "aging model" we live with. In those ways, we often show our fear of the truth that time is passing and we're mortal after all.

As a society, we tend to mask the effects of injustice by distancing ourselves from those who suffer under it. Perhaps we project laziness or genetic deficiencies on those who are deprived of basic opportunities. Then we show our fear of the truth that we might help others, but simply refuse to move out of our comfort zones.

As a society, we tend to mask the effects of lapsed spirituality by claiming there is no God, or that we're all God. We replace corporate worship with corporate indifference. We squeeze every possible gratification out of this moment rather than take any thought for the future in this life or eternity. And we run away from the truth that God may well be watching us, grieving over us—and in rare moments, even rejoicing with us.

But we never invite him to the party.

As a society, we wear character masks of what we want to be rather than what we are. We claim to admire accountability—but only for the other guy. "We hold these truths to be self-evident"—as long as they're self-serving. We want to be like Mother Teresa or Billy Graham, so we put them on television specials— we can have a virtual experience of their lives of service while we munch popcorn on our sofas. And we dodge the truth that we're too cowardly to put ourselves at the kind of risk that could actually build character in us.

Society's Character

If we think back through the issues we have covered in this book and analyze each of them in a broader sense, what we find is that we have covered issues on a personal level that lead to many of the problems we face together as a society.

What are the social problems that stem from the lack of integrity, honesty, and truth-telling in our society? Here are just a few examples.

We have failed to tell our children and youth the truth about developing healthy relationships and moral responsibility. We have covered up the failure of our generation to live with sexual purity by giving permission to our children to freely experiment with the dynamite that nearly destroyed us. Sex without commitment is now our cultural expectation, and we have prostituted our children to ease our own consciences.

We have failed to tell ourselves the truth about the effects of violence as entertainment. We act shocked when we hear of a child shooting a classmate, but smile with approval when the same child blows the head off a video foe. We put on a mask of disgust when we hear of a violent murder, but tune in to see the graphic details on the evening news—and the tabloid TV show after the news. Virtual violence has led us to make less of the real thing, victims notwithstanding.

We have failed to tell ourselves at work that there's honor in doing the right thing even at the expense of profit margins and the "good old boy" network. Qualified candidates are still too often denied a position of leadership if they don't meet up with a company's longstanding, if assumed, gender or racial expectations. From telephone service "slamming" to tobacco study manipulations, we put human dignity at risk in exchange for another buck. Treating customers and donors like people instead of dollar signs is becoming a lost art, and trust is eroding as a result.

In the last few decades, from Richard Nixon to Bill Clinton, the integrity of the highest office in our country has been assaulted. Events surrounding the last few years of the Clinton presidency and the congressional response to it form, of course, a "big example" from recent history. Why? We don't need to dig into the details of the whole sordid mess. But the bottom line is that the president of the United States—and then a succession of public officials—were caught in lies.

Political Truth: An Oxymoron, or a Reasonable Expectation?

When challenged about having had a sexual relationship with an intern, President Clinton denied having "sexual relations with that woman, Ms. Lewinsky." We came to find out over the ensuing months that we had a president who, rather than owning up to something that any reasonable person would accept as "inappropriate sexual contact," began to manipulate the meaning of his words. By using words that could only be described as pliable, moldable, able to accommodate whatever linguistic machinations were needed, the president set course to navigate around future questions. In so doing, he brought new attention to the grade-school English exercise of parsing.

From one perspective, the president's parsing could be looked at as a clever and precise use of language. From another, it clearly was verbal misdirection. Words took on rather arcane meanings. We couldn't listen to the president any longer without asking ourselves what technical meaning he was applying to each word in his statements.

One consequence of all this was that the venom of a large segment of the nation was turned against Clinton. Cries of immorality rose from all points around our nation.

On the political right, many strong and self-righteous claims were made about the kind of leadership Bill Clinton could offer in light of, first, his moral failing and, second, his deceit and language games to avoid taking responsibility.

From the political left came tortured logic, some of which condoned the president's actions. The argument was that the moral failure was personal, not political. Further, that the precise use of language was just that, precise, and not intended to deceive.

The conflict grew in intensity and in the heated execution of arguments on both sides.

Perhaps the best thing that can be said of this situation is that it confirms to us that emotional leprosy is rampant. And if nothing else, this painful time in

American history allowed some people to begin to feel again, to have their nerves come alive and feel the pain that warns us of trouble with our moral character.

We heard a lot about the Rule of Law during this episode. As we mentioned much earlier, this means that the law is no respecter of persons; it's a power unto itself, and no one can rise above it or subvert it. What we didn't hear much of was talk of the Rule of Truth. (Okay, we made up the name, but discussion of the principle was sadly lacking anyway.)

In fact, what played out in our nation's capital was not unlike the story we discussed in chapter 2. There, we recounted the Bible story in which the religious leaders brought the woman caught in adultery before Jesus.

The "facts" of the religious leaders' case were essentially undisputed. That's much the same as the facts of the case against President Clinton, once they were all made public. But the religious leaders' intent in telling the truth was wrong. They intended the truth to be something that would put Jesus into a position that was at least untenable, if not unwinnable. In the case of the president, many of his political opponents intended the truth to be a weapon, something to destroy a political enemy who had already aroused much hatred. The president's acts with an intern, as despicable as they were, didn't create the furor against him. The opportunity for the president's enemies to use this against him — to vent all of their hostility toward him, to remove him from the Washington game — created the furor.

Certainly, we're not going to continue comparing Bill Clinton to Jesus in this situation. As far as moral culpability based on the facts, the comparison stands to be made between the president and the woman caught in adultery. Jesus stood before the religious leaders innocent and legally detached from the facts of their case.

What we're doing, however, is comparing the way the religious leaders of Jesus' time used truth as a weapon and the way the many anti-Clinton interest groups used the truth of the president's misdeeds as a weapon. Not all of the moral outrage we heard over the airwaves was pure concern for the morality of our country. The situation was often used as a political expediency to cripple a foe found in a president that many had come to hate.

How do we come to this conclusion? It's simple. Was the concept of the Rule of Truth used in addressing this issue? How might it have been applied to effect a different tone in dealing with the scandal, results notwithstanding?

It was far too easy for many opponents of the president to point out his shortcomings without taking that same moral lens to themselves. Issues and situations that could have been subject to the same scrutiny they brought to the president's situation continued without correction. It was, and continues to be, as though moral accountability—much less a moral overhaul—isn't necessary unless it's politically expedient.

This only added weight to the argument made by Clinton supporters that the uproar had nothing to do with the need for public leaders to travel the high road of truth. In fact, when the mudslinging continued and began to hit figures on both sides of the political aisle, the response seemed to be that mudslinging was a greater character issue than the inability of public figures to deal with the truth about themselves.

A Hero in the Fray

We found one particularly poignant and telling moment, however, as the impeachment process drew closer to a House vote. Representative Bob Livingston of Louisiana removed himself from the short list of candidates to take over the role of Speaker of the House. Livingston wanted both to curb the mudslinging and to take responsibility for his past miscues as a family man. He could have grabbed at a power position with a "Look, everybody's got skeletons in the closet, so let's forget about this" attitude. Instead, he committed to do the hard work of facing the truth about himself, which meant giving more attention to his family and less to his political future.

It was fascinating to hear the hue and cry of the response to Livingston's decision. A surprising number of the president's supporters called for Livingston to rescind his decision and put his hat back in the ring of Speaker candidates. They seemed to understand that Livingston's action poured new light on their fatal, relativist mistakes.

There were those among the president's supporters who saw nothing wrong with an extramarital fling with an intern in the first place. They claimed that one's private life has no effect on one's public character; therefore, private morality has no place in a public forum. In fact, the president's supporters wanted to assure the nation that such was the case. What do marriage vows have to do with an oath of office, anyway?

Setting politics aside, and looking simply at Livingston's application of the Rule of Truth to himself, Livingston made the ultimate argument against their reasoning. In effect, he said private promises *are* crucial to public character—and there is more to life than power-grabbing. There's a correct way to handle truth.

Build a Society: Can You Bypass People?

The infections that plagued our government in that situation, and that plague us as a society now, are born out of the sustained and progressive loss of feeling for moral responsibility that we have as individuals. What is society, after all, if not a collection of individuals? And as individuals we've worked at removing pain from our lives personally, professionally, and in our society.

Contrary to popular belief, it's not these big events that tear the nation apart. It's the details, the small choices, and the small compromises we make with truth in our everyday lives that bring us to this place.

This place is one where we know people are pilfering things from work and we don't confront them because it will be uncomfortable, maybe even cost someone's job. It's the place where people refuse to stand up for truth when a crime has been committed, for fear of retribution. It's the place we each visit where family and friends are involved in self-destructive behavior and we know something has to be done, but we don't want the emotional trauma or the conflict in our lives. It's when we choose to accept the absence of pain over truth and health.

You May Be Right: I Might Be Crazy

Only about a third of those surveyed believe strongly that "whatever works best for you is the only truth you can know."[1] Nearly half of us believe strongly that the Bible provides us with absolute moral truths that apply to everyone, with another 18 percent agreeing "somewhat."[2]

What's the answer to our cultural dilemma? A great social outcry to bring morals back into the public discussion? Courses in ethics for everyone in public service? Hanging the Ten Commandments in every school? It isn't likely these in themselves can bring about the difference many of us are looking for.

The change will come when we begin to assume our responsibility as citizens. The seeds that transform will be planted as we speak out in truth and love about the things that we see are going wrong, not just in the public sector, but in our personal lives first.

We must restore character to every avenue of life. We must raise children who have no fear of speaking the truth. We must work to hold ourselves accountable for using truth as something that enhances growth and development, not as a weapon to be used to bludgeon our enemies.

We've mentioned before our religious faith—that we're Christians. We like the short, smart phrase the Bible gives us as the key to telling the truth on a daily basis. It reminds us that every small decision for truth-telling and truth-hearing will affect our families, our workplaces, and our society. Jesus' words are recorded in Luke 16:10:

> "Whoever can be trusted with very little can also be trusted with very much, and whoever is dishonest with very little will also be dishonest with much."

The everyday and private decisions *do* impact the more public roles we have in life. Our answer for restoring integrity in everyday life is not found in the large crisis. The crisis itself is but a symptom. The answer is in the everyday practice of truth-telling, integrity, and accountability. As we start small and are faithful in the small things, then we will see progress at a more visible level in our society.

To make this into a statement of faith, we believe that God is in these details. And as we take care to exercise truth in everyday life, he will honor our efforts.

That's why the illustrations we use in this book and the insights we give into telling the truth, no matter the venue they occur in, are personal, individual stories. They're about the everyday—not the ethics of the exception, not the logical extrapolation of concepts until they break. They're about encouraging the valor necessary for people to stand up, to be willing—even anxious—for the positive pain and healing that come with telling the truth. We must each wake up, come alive, and work at staying alive, not slipping into the anesthetizing pool of "truth decay"[3] our society has told us is so healthy.

There's a risk in this tactic. People may actually regard truth-telling as somewhat crazy in the everyday business of life. They might think you're a bit off your rocker when you practice truth-telling. So don't be surprised. But in a society uncertain of truth as a tool for life and character development, looking a bit— maybe a lot—different from the approved cultural norm might not be such a bad thing. French theorist Antonin Artaud put it this way:

> And what is an authentic madman? It's a man who preferred to become mad, in the socially accepted sense of the word, rather than forfeit a certain superior idea of human honor. . . . For a madman is also a man whom society did not want to hear and whom it wanted to prevent from uttering certain intolerable truths.[4]

Life is hard. There is pain. From pain comes growth. Growth produces character. Character produces people who fearlessly pursue truth in themselves, in others, and in our society.

We have our own struggles with character. We're not above the fray. But we continue to learn that applying the Rule of Truth to ourselves only helps us grow.

Our masks reveal our fear of the truth. If a society is to survive, it must become more than a masked ball. At the risk of being different—even being called crazy—it's time to pursue the higher honor.

section
three

embracing truth in a culture of lies

the truth: sooner rather than later the truth: sooner rather than later the truth: sooner rather than later the truth: sooner rather than later the truth: sooner rather than later the truth: sooner rather than later the truth: sooner rather than later the truth: sooner rather than later

Chapter

9 ▶ the truth:

sooner rather than later

When we're planning for posterity, we ought to remember that virtue is not hereditary.
—Thomas Paine

The tractor of choice on the small Iowa acreage where Steve was raised was a small 1952 Ford. It was sized halfway between a garden tractor and a larger open-seat (no cab) model.

Steve's dad, Don, knew that machine inside and out. By the time Steve left the family homestead for college, his dad and grandfather had pretty much rebuilt the tractor at least once, maybe twice.

Don was determined that Steve know what it took to make the tractor run. Patiently, over time, by starting Steve young and working alongside him, Don taught him how to switch towing drawbars, clean the related machinery, rebuild the glass bubble carburetor, change the spark plugs, check the tire pressure, drive the thing and, of course, check the oil and gas.

Mechanics was not a natural gift for Steve. Yet he garnered enough experience with tools not only to effectively run the tractor, but also to translate his developed skills with tools into fencing, roofing, and framing work in the years to come.

Meanwhile in Ohio, Bob Donaldson just knew his son would someday mow lawns for money. There was a trusty, yet sporty, green and silver mower in the garage just right for the purpose. So Bob taught Devlin the ins and outs of the family Lawn Boy: restringing the pull-start rope, cleaning and changing the spark plug, monitoring the spark plug wire, tightening the wheels, cleaning the underside of the mower, running it safely, and, of course, checking the oil and gas.

Devlin's natural aptitude for mechanics wouldn't have qualified him for an Indy pit crew. But Bob stuck with the process with patience. Devlin emerged from the training familiar with the proper way to use tools, which led to bigger and better paychecks as a drywaller and painter in later life.

Please note this: At no time did Don Wamberg or Bob Donaldson *assume* their sons would somehow innately develop the skills for handling tools. The fathers *showed* their sons what to do.

This is crucial to note because sometimes it seems we have abdicated our roles of showing the next generation the tools of truth.

What Are We Passing On?

We dedicated this book to our fathers because they modeled truth for us. They took the time to discuss the benefits and risks of truth-telling, and they never let us off the hook regarding truth: it was as much of a requirement in everyday life as breathing.

That's not to say we succeeded in truth-telling at every opportunity. Many times we failed miserably. Yet our dads instilled in us the kind of conscience that wouldn't allow us to rest comfortably in the context of a lie.

The idea of moral conscience was usually reinforced by the media of the day. We remember a complete *TV Guide* listing for an episode of *Leave It to Beaver* saying something like "Beaver tells a lie." Our parents could let us loose on that half-hour episode in full confidence that there would be consequences and a lesson learned by "The Beav" that would reinforce the importance of truth.

Contrast that to today. Bringing up the sore subject of the last chapter, nearly a year passed as the importance of truth was undermined daily for the sake of politics. Standards of conduct were redefined publicly. Our society saw that you could lie about sex and get away with it—and then that if you were caught in the lie, you could redefine terms so you weren't really lying after all.

There's a painful consequence to that phenomenon. Some teenagers took the president's redefinition of "sexual relations" and put it into practice for themselves. "Hey, the president says oral sex really doesn't count!" Even among some of the church youth groups we're familiar with, there was a marked increase in such sexual experimentation due to the newly revised standards.

We know the common argument that teenagers will experiment with sex at some time anyway. We probably sound like prudes to even mention this. But what bothers us is that the president effectively caused the ethics of his exception to become the ethics of the everyday for some impressionable kids. And hundreds of public officials defended his choice to do so.

What are we passing on to our children? Will we leave their views on the truth to whatever they pick up from the culture? Or will we patiently work with them to intentionally develop their skills with the truth?

It's a challenge we must face. But let's start with some perspective on what the next generation is thinking about truth.

The "Read" on Truth

The Barna Research Group has conducted an extensive survey of teenagers on issues of truth and ethics. Some of the questions were identical to those asked of adults in other surveys; others focused on teenage-specific issues.

The teenagers, aged thirteen through eighteen, believed integrity to be a desirable personal characteristic. Just over 90 percent of those surveyed said "living with a high degree of integrity" was very or somewhat desirable for their futures.[1] Teenagers who discussed faith weekly, discussed values weekly, or who completely accepted the truth as being absolute had appreciably higher scores as groups who perceived living with a very high degree of integrity to be "very desirable."[2] Participation in religious training also seemed to bring the scores up. Teenagers who read the Bible at least weekly, took part in a weekly Bible study or youth group, or attended Sunday school or church weekly were about 10 percent more likely to think that living with a high degree of integrity was "very important."[3]

That being said, only one-half of one percent thought "the state of youth morals" was one of the two or three problems that most concerned them. Educational concerns far outweighed moral and spiritual concerns.[4]

Integrity matters to these teenagers. But upon what standards will they build their integrity? Over 70 percent of the same respondents agreed with this statement: "There is no such thing as 'absolute truth'; two people could define 'truth' in conflicting ways and both could still be correct."[5] The number dropped to under 60 percent in agreement among teenagers who identified themselves as "born again," and to just over 40 percent for those who identified themselves as "evangelical."[6] The number rises to 90 percent among teenagers using drugs, and to over 80 percent among those who are sexually active.[7]

Could this be a signal that how someone handles the truth really does affect his behavior? And, among our youth, that an "it doesn't matter" attitude toward absolutes might be leading to an "it doesn't matter" attitude toward potentially self-destructive behavior?

We're still haunted by memories of a friend of ours from college days who, embittered by a broken engagement, threw himself into a pattern of extreme drug abuse and outright sexual perversion. "When I lived my life by the book, I ended up with a broken heart. So those rules don't apply to me anymore," was Mitch's constant litany. Absolutes didn't matter to Mitch anymore. It really wasn't that big of a step to life not mattering anymore.

Within ten years, Mitch was gone. Dead. There's no happy ending to this story. He disappeared from our maps. He didn't want to be in touch with anyone "who knew him when . . . " We still ask ourselves every now and then what we could have done, what we would have done if given the chance.

About the only thing we've come up with fifteen years after the fact is that we would have reminded him, with words and deeds, of the truth that his life mattered both to us and to God.

What are we telling our children? That they take second place to our schedules, our jobs, our dreams? That their actions will have no consequences? That they'll be able to talk their way out of any trouble? Or are we telling them that who they are and what they do matters deeply to us and to God?

Have we explained truth well enough to give our children a clear idea of what it looks like and how it can be defined? The answer to that question is still unclear. Eighty percent of teenagers surveyed agreed with the statement "When it comes to matters of morals and ethics, truth means different things to different people; no one can be absolutely positive that they know the truth."[8] Again, religious perspective changed the numbers. Among teenagers who identified themselves as "born again," the number who agreed with the statement dropped to 66 percent. Less than half—only 42 percent—of teenagers who called themselves "evangelical" agreed with the statement.[9]

But there is still the sense that "truth" is a slippery thing to grab hold of and apply, even if you believe in some sort of objective truth. More than 90 percent of teenagers surveyed agreed with the statement "What is right for one person in a given situation might not be right for another person in a similar situation."[10] And this time, the numbers didn't change appreciably for teenagers identifying themselves as "born again" or "evangelical."[11]

This could mean that teenagers don't know how to apply the principles of truth and morality to everyday life. They may still struggle with making the ethics of the exception into the ethics of the everyday.

Sadly, they have plenty of adult role models in the culture who will show them how to do just that.

The Challenge

So what can we learn from the above?

Frankly, there aren't too many surprises. The next generation has perceptions about the truth very similar to ours. Truth and integrity are perceived as highly positive values, for example. They're just tough—and sadly, may be perceived as increasingly impossible—to live out.

Where are the signs of hope in all this? Not surprisingly, the teenagers who had regular discussions about values and faith had more-positive responses toward truth and the need to actually integrate absolutes into life. Teenagers who practiced regular Bible reading and church participation also responded more favorably to the idea of absolutes that mattered.

Our challenge lies here: It seems the next generation has picked up on our own insecurities with talking about truth in terms of absolutes. We seem, as a culture, to have done a masterful job of arguing the ethics of the exception into being the ethics of the everyday. Suspend all belief and authenticate yourself through action—even if that action has no basis in seeking good for yourself or others. Today's absolute just might go out of fashion tomorrow, so why be picky about absolutes?

What can we do to secure the future of truth for generations to come?

Action Items

We're not here to create a list of impossible demands on building the truth into the next generation. But here are four things you can do to help.

1. Talk regularly with the children in your life about faith and values, including the importance of truth. Whether you're a parent, a Sunday school teacher, or a next-door neighbor, help the children around you understand that truth matters. Help them understand how truth benefits trust-building in relationships.

Brent noticed some change missing from his dresser one afternoon. He also noticed his six-year-old son, Joey, wiping off the remnants of a king-sized candy bar when Joey returned from a trip to the supermarket with his mother.

It was okay for Joey to have candy bars occasionally, but only with his own money. Brent had seen Joey spend his allowance on a small toy the weekend before. So Brent checked with Margo, his wife. Joey had told Margo that he had his own money for the candy bar. Brent confronted Joey gently, eye to eye.

"Son, did you take money from my dresser for the candy bar you ate today?" Joey's mouth dropped wide open. He nodded slowly.

"Joey, you lied to your mom about where that money came from, didn't you?" Another nod came from Joey.

"If you'd have asked, I might have given you the money anyway. But now you've stolen from me. Then you lied about it to Mom. That makes it hard for me to trust you like I once did.

"But I want you to know something: I'll never lie to you because I want you to trust me. And you can help me trust you more by telling the truth to everyone, especially everyone in our family. That's what we expect. Will you try to do that?"

Brent didn't explode. He just laid out the terms of the family's social contract.

2. Be truthful and trustworthy in your relationships with the children you influence. One of the basic principles of life is that truth between people builds trust. Model it. Follow through on your promises. (That's our special reminder for dads like us who too often worry more about time cutting a business deal than time at soccer games and piano recitals. Enough said.)

"Mrs. Smith, you said you'd let us have recess outside if we all finished our math."

"Mom, you promised you'd help me with this home economics project."

"Mr. Rawlings, you said we could have a pizza party with the extra money we made from our fundraiser."

"Dad, you said you were taking me to the football game today. Why aren't you getting ready?"

We understand. We'd like the kids in our lives to listen just as well to our desires as they do for the things they want us to do. But to win that kind of respect, we need to deliver on our promises and appointments.

3. Share your stories of truth and its impact on your life. We seem to have forgotten how to tell our stories to the next generation. The assumption—almost universally wrong—is that our children aren't interested in what we've learned from life. But when you put life's lessons into the context of a story from your life, you might be surprised at how receptive your "audience" becomes. (Don't forget to include in the mix current stories from the workplace or stories about what you encounter in the culture.)

Steve's grandfather Roy told each of his seven grandchildren his story about being caught smoking a cigar behind the chicken coop. He was nine at the time of the incident.

Roy had planned the event for a time when he was sure his father would be away from the farm. Instead, just a few puffs into the cigar, Roy heard heavy and familiar footsteps coming his way. Roy's response to the moment of crisis was to hide the still-lit cigar behind his back.

"Roy, is something burning?"

"I don't know, Dad."

Thomas Jefferson Knopp was no fool. He could see the smoke coming from behind his son's back, and it wasn't exactly forming a halo around Roy's head at the moment.

"Smells like a cigar to me. Where did you get it?"

"What? A cigar?"

That was a big mistake. "T. J." Knopp hated lying with a passion. He called Roy on the carpet, and as punishment, made Roy finish smoking the cigar, which he did.

When Roy retold this story to his grandchildren, he was wide open about how he plotted to steal a cigar from his father's supply, how he thought he chose a time when his father wouldn't be around to catch him, how grown-up he felt when he first lit the cigar, how sick he became when he finished it under his father's watchful eye—and how stupid it was to lie. Roy spun a wonderful tale, but the most important thing was that his grandchildren heard the tale face to face. It was a story of when Grandpa was a kid himself, and a lesson learned about truth-telling. That, more than anything else, made it memorable to the grandkids.

4. Take the children you influence to church. Read the Bible with them, too. The statistics don't lie: Kids engaged in regular religious training are friendlier toward issues of truth and absolutes. They also need to see that the church and the Bible are sources of ethical and moral encouragement for you, too.

For us, the people who make up our spiritual families are crucial in reinforcing positive values, including truth-telling, in our children. We both also work hard to be positive examples for other peoples' children at church.

The training our children receive at church opens the door for talks about the importance of the truth and about our belief that the Bible is an important source of truth for everyday life. It's been a genuine kick to share the stories we love in the Bible with our kids, and to remind them that they apply to real life.

Back to the Bottom Line

As we prepare upcoming generations to fill our shoes, we have to apply the Rule of Truth: we must put the lens of truth on our own ideas and actions before we can give them the tools to "do the truth."

The next generations need to see how truth can be integrated into workplaces filled with political machinations. They need to witness how truth can benefit marriages and parenting alike. They need to experience the benefits of truth, whether it's well-deserved praise or a simple thank-you for doing the right thing.

They need to know you tell the truth to help them, not to keep them from developing their God-given potential. They need to embrace the pain of hearing the truth and to be shown appropriate ways to act on it.

It's not so different from when we watched our dads turn a bolt right before they handed the crescent wrench to us to take our turn. We trusted that they were showing us how to use a tool correctly—and when the machine fired up and ran, just as they had told us it would, we knew they were.

the overview: fourteen tactics to restore integrity to everyday life the overview: fourteen tactics to restore integrity to everyday life the overview: fourteen tactics to restore integrity to everyday life the overview: fourteen tactics to restore integrity to everyday life the overview: fourteen tactics to restore integrity to everyday life the overview: fourteen tactics to restore

Chapter

the overview

fourteen tactics to restore integrity to everyday life

Truth is the cry of all, but the game of the few.
—George Berkeley

O nce there was a missionary—let's call her Clara—who served in an African village. For years, Clara felt she had achieved great success in communicating the principles of her faith to the local people.

The problem was, she never really noticed their behavior changing. This troubled Clara, as you might expect, so she took the time one afternoon to talk with some of the women in the village as they were preparing a communal meal.

"Sylvia," the missionary began, "I am your friend, am I not?"

The wife of the local chief smiled. "Of course you are." She cocked her head to one side as she surveyed the face of the faithful missionary. "Why do you ask?"

"It seems as though I'm not having an impact on your everyday lives. In fact, it seems to me sometimes that I've wasted all these years here."

"What makes you say that?"

"Simply the way you live life each day. You come to church on Sundays, you seem to agree with what I say, and I appreciate that. But during the week, many of the villagers still visit the local medicine man. Some of them still make sacrifices to the local gods. I even baptized some of you. So what should I do to help your commitment become a carryover into everyday life?"

"There is something you could do. You ask us to agree with you about God. Perhaps now you need to tell us something about how he wants us to live each day. Our medicine man tells us what he expects in our everyday lives. He tells us exactly what we need to do to please the gods—very practical things. I do agree with you about how wonderful your God is, Clara. But it doesn't seem that he wants to bother much with our everyday lives. Maybe you could tell us what he expects us to do. Could you do that?"

The rest of the local women gathered around nodded their agreement.

Clara was surprised. She had communicated the principles of her faith well, but for many years had forgotten how important it was to let people know about the everyday tactics of her faith.

We won't give you a course on missionary outreach right now. But we're well aware that we'd be less than helpful if we failed to give you a number of practical hints that could help you make truth-telling an everyday habit. That's why we're including this overview. We want to give you the tools that will actually help you tell the truth consistently, regardless of the cost.

We unpacked each of these tactics as we went through the book. But now, we want to present them all together. We think it's important that you have a way to review these tactics in one setting. So let's start now.

Tactic 1: Understand the Power of Words

Language has limits. What you say—and what you don't say—affects the way the truth you want to tell is understood.

There are three simple realities about language, garnered from generations of research from people who study the nature of language. They're not magic. We want to review those now:

1. The word is not the thing. This simply means that language is language, and not the reality it describes. When you tell the truth, you need to understand that your own words mean nothing without the reality to back them up.

2. You can't say everything about anything. Do you remember the old phrase "the truth, the whole truth, and nothing but the truth"? There's a problem with saying "the whole truth." It's only the whole truth as best you can tell it—and you can tell nothing but the truth. But there's no way one observer can say everything about anything.

3. You can end up talking about talking. One of the limitations of language is that, indeed, you can say a whole lot about nothing. Just because something is put into words doesn't necessarily mean it's significant.

It all boils down to this: The very nature of language should be enough to humble the boldest truth-teller among us. It should serve to remind us that as perfect as our understanding may be, the way we express it will not be perfect.

Tactic 2: If There's a Problem, Say So

Sometimes people complain that our society is far too vulgar. In many ways, we agree. And yet when it comes to the truth, it seems to us that we're far too polite. In fact, we're cowards.

What do we do when we see a problem? Are we willing to address it forthrightly, or do we prefer to let it go *ad infinitum, ad nauseum* for the sake of convenience?

Some of us even put off confronting our children over problems we see in their behavior. It isn't appropriate for children to develop a built-in expectation that they'll get everything they want, whether it's in a grocery store aisle or in the car as your family decides which restaurant will be serving you lunch. Children have to learn to deal with not always getting their own way. Yet instead of dealing with pouting and whining—and a subsequent responsibility to call such behavior into account—parents often give in to save their energy for another battle.

That's a bad idea. What happens when your child finally has to decide these issues with friends, or with friends and their families? Our refusal to deal truthfully with an issue this simple, this basic to the social contract, is setting up our children to fail miserably in relationships with others.

We're not saying that taking on this challenge is easy. As parents, we face this issue almost daily. But let's not mistake our unwillingness to tell someone a difficult truth for kindness. In the same light, we shouldn't mistake our desire to tell someone a difficult truth for charity, either.

We have to take the responsibility upon ourselves to tell the truth when we see a problem. We don't need to make more of the problem than it is. But we must be sure that what begins as a small problem doesn't grow into a huge one—and that the huge problem doesn't become dangerous to the integrity of our home, workplace, or society.

Tactic 3: If There's Not a Problem, Say So

And then there are those of us who want to see trouble when no trouble is there. That makes it twice as important for those of us who see there *is* no trouble to make that known.

As Mary approached middle age, she was convinced her husband, Jim, was slowly but surely "falling out of love" with her. The small talk they once shared had dwindled to the nonexistent level. Jim seemed to wander around the house with his temperament set on slow boil. His sense of humor—the character trait that had first drawn Mary to Jim—was nowhere to be found on the home front.

Mary immediately assumed that, somehow, she was the problem. She went through a few weeks of self-assessment, then self-condemnation about all the things she must be neglecting to put Jim in this constant mood. She began to lose weight. She kept the house spotless. She cooked up a storm. Jim commented now and then with appreciation and encouragement, but there was no denying that he was still stewing about something.

Finally Jim said, "Honey, are you okay? This is really great. The house looks a lot better. You're taking better care of yourself. I love coming home to a hot meal. But are you wearing yourself out? Do you need to slow down a bit? There's no reason that *both* of us should be burning out here."

"*Both* of us? What do you mean?"

"Aw, work has just been brutal the last few months. I haven't said anything because I didn't want to worry you."

But the truth is, not saying anything produced more worry in Mary than an explanation would have.

A wife may assume that her husband is thinking about leaving her, when he is simply preoccupied with a difficult time on the job. On the flip side, a worker may falsely believe his job is on the line when his boss is having a rough time at home. Young children rarely get over a conflict with a parent as quickly as the parent does.

In each of these cases, the truth is clearly a healer. And the sooner the truth is told, the better. It needs to be brought to light as quickly as possible to avoid further misunderstanding and possible hurt in those who need to hear it. So do yourself and the people around you a big favor: If there's no problem between you and them, let them know. The same goes for a "no-problem" analysis from you regarding another's performance on the job, at home, in a friendship, or even in church.

"No problem" is usually good news, isn't it? Then it's news worth mentioning.

Tactic 4: Clarify, Don't Mollify

So you've decided to take on the responsibility of telling the truth in a difficult situation. You're about to enter into one of the most delicate areas of truth-telling.

Misty was patently offensive when she talked to most people. She constantly interrupted others in conversation. And once she began talking, she refused to take a breath deep enough to let someone else share in the discussion.

Margo watched for some weeks while others physically avoided Misty in the cafeteria at work. Finally, she made the decision to let Misty know how she was perceived by their coworkers.

It took Margo three tries to get her point across. She tried to begin slowly. "Misty, I want to talk to you about something."

And Misty was off to the races. "Isn't it great to have someone to talk to? I've really had problems getting anyone to talk to me recently. . . . "

Margo stopped Misty cold in her verbal tracks. "And that's what I want to talk to you about. You need to listen to me."

Misty started in again. "Oh, that's really important, to listen, isn't it? I know I feel a lot better when people listen to me and . . . "

At this instant, Margo could have let Misty continue as she had previously during the years of their friendship. This time, however, she said gently but with intensity, *"Stop talking right now. Don't open your mouth until I tell you to.* Think about what we've just done. I've tried to talk, and you haven't let me. That's why our friends here are avoiding you these days."

Margo was able to make her point, and then help Misty carry on real give-and-take conversations in the cafeteria at work in the months that followed. We have to admire Margo's persistence on behalf of her friend, and her determination to tell Misty the truth.

It's only human nature to desire to ease the burden for the sake of the person you're talking to. Don't do it. Yes, we still want you to be kind, but we don't want you to be so kind that you neutralize another's need to recognize and act upon the truth you're telling.

And be clear about the problem. It's usually best not to delve into a complicated history about why things are the way they are. It's much better to deal with the present, clarify what needs to be corrected, and offer your encouragement toward that end. Then you can backtrack to the history if the problem—and the truth—call for that.

Tactic 5: Clarify, Don't Smear

There's another perspective to consider when you clarify. Don't let your feelings surrounding a situation cloud the truth. Be sure that you deal with facts rather than opinions and emotions.

We have to be especially careful when our feelings may tend to paint someone else as a villain in a given situation. It can be tempting to make someone else a scapegoat when things get tough. In our attempts to help someone accept the truth, it's easy to create an opening with that person by laying the blame for the situation on someone else.

You know the drill. Ryan is a constant source of conflict on your company's social committee. When Jeff responds in anger to one of Ryan's snide comments, the common response may be "Ryan deserved it." The thinking goes like this: "I know we were only responding to what Ryan did. None of us should be in this position. You can't really blame yourself for your actions. Any one of us would've lost our temper."

Well, the truth of the matter is that "any one of us" in this situation did *not* lose his temper. Jeff *did* lose his temper. And that's the rub: We can't blame Ryan for someone else's temper tantrum. We have to help the person with a temper problem take responsibility for his actions.

The bottom line here? Truth is best served by clarifying who is responsible for inappropriate action. There may be underlying causes—causes that may even seem to be justified—for someone's action. But the situation is only clarified when those responsible for negative actions are individually confronted with *their* responsibility, no matter how others have acted.

Tactic 6: Give Credit Where It's Due

Are you a "gusher"? Do you compliment people to the extent that they no longer believe you're offering genuine praise for an accomplishment? Or are you a stoic—someone who refuses to say "Good job!" to a child or a colleague simply because you expect a certain standard of performance?

In either case this tactic of truth will do you some good. It takes discipline to give credit where credit's due. The discipline involves the facts surrounding a job well done. Your mission, should you decide to accept it, is to tie a compliment to the facts. Nothing more, nothing less.

"Jon, you did a dynamite job on that math test. Bringing your grade up from a D to a B is wonderful!"

"Simone, your presentation in the meeting this morning was crystal clear. I thought the handouts you provided kept everyone focused. For once, I didn't feel that we were wasting company time eating donuts in a closed room. Thanks!"

This tactic is a key to encouragement that matters. A child who hears a specific compliment based on a job well done—school work, chores at home, getting along with his sister—is on his way to repeating that positive behavior. A colleague who hears your gratitude for her part in making your job easier will feel better about you, your relationship, and likely the place where you both work.

One last thing: When was the last time you gave credit to your spouse for a job well done on the home front?

Tactic 7: Give Correction Where It's Due

This may seem to repeat the "Clarify, Don't . . . " points above (tactics 4 and 5). While there's a natural connection with these points, their application could be different. The points above are about *clearly confronting and assigning responsibility* in a difficult situation. This point is about *offering correction,* giving practical advice on how to make things better.

This should be fairly easy. As it is with giving credit where credit's due, giving correction involves the discipline of dealing with facts. So, one more time: Your mission, should you decide to accept it, is to tie correction to the facts. Nothing more, nothing less.

"Jon, it looks like you have some work to do on math. It seems to me from this test that you're having a problem understanding fractions—especially improper fractions. Let's talk about those, and see if I can help you understand them better." (If not, there's a reason we pay teachers.)

"Simone, the amount of time you spend around the water cooler gives some people around here the impression that you're not working hard. I'm satisfied with your effort, but perhaps you should cut down on the time you spend in the break room. It's giving a false impression to some people who really look up to you."

This tactic is key—even crucial—in giving coaching or correction that matters. A child who receives correction based on facts—mistakes in homework, chores left undone, arguments with the siblings—is receiving the information he needs to avoid problems in the future. And a colleague who hears practical hints from you on how to be a better coworker will often end up thanking you for your investment in her future.

Remember this, too: once you start giving correction, you'd better be ready to receive it.

Tactic 8: Talk to the Source of Your Problem

We've already dealt with the need to tell the truth about the people and problems around us. Now we need to talk about something else: One of the most important tactics of telling the truth is to deal honestly with our problems. More often than not, this means we have to speak honestly to ourselves. In other cases, it means we have to speak honestly to others who contribute to our problems.

Understand this, please: This tactic is not about blaming someone else. This tactic is about doing what's needed to make a relationship better.

Suppose Sherry, your close friend, is consistently late for the carpool to work. Her inability to be on time affects your ability to get to work on time. In earlier days, when you were late for college classes, it wasn't as big a deal. But now a paycheck is on the line—and not just her paycheck, but your paycheck, too. You need Sherry to be on time for the carpool.

Sherry keeps showing up late. You, keeping silence to preserve your friendship, are about to develop an ulcer. You're barely able to contain your anger whenever you see Sherry. So, what do you think—is it time to talk to the source of your problem?

We hope so, because in reality, your friendship with Sherry depends on this conversation. To keep your relationship alive, you need to talk to her about the problem she's creating for you.

At the same time, we hope you remember that Sherry isn't at all responsible for your inability to turn down that second piece of chocolate cake. That's a conversation you must have with yourself.

Tactic 9: Recognize the Sources of Your Success

We believe that the "self-made man"—or the self-made woman—is a myth. One of the most important tactics of telling the truth, then, is to recognize the sources of your success.

This tactic will not only keep you humble, but also will keep your thank-you list current. It's not an exercise in false humility. Rather, it's an honest recognition that others have contributed to the positive events in your life.

Sometimes it's tempting to keep all the credit for a personal success. Other times, it's just as tempting to turn down an honest compliment when you really deserve it. In either case, your personal integrity is compromised. You're not telling the truth, or perhaps not hearing the truth, about yourself.

One of the best things to do in cases like these is to recognize the contributions of others. Take an honest tally of all the people who've helped you achieve your success. Maybe your third-grade teacher had a hand in who you are. Perhaps a Little League coach taught you a valuable character lesson. Most of us can thank one or both parents for some positive aspects of our lives. Maybe a colleague at work gave you crucial insight to better predict next quarter's sales curve.

Whatever the case, let others know about the people who helped you along the way.

Tactic 10: Tact Doesn't Equal Little White Lies

How do you let someone know you disagree with her without hurting her feelings? Many of us choose not to let others know at all. Sometimes we keep silent. And other times we dodge a disagreement with verbal distractions.

Society calls these distractions "little white lies." Common wisdom says you tell these lies to avoid the greater evil of hurting someone's feelings. We believe tact calls for different tactics.

Suppose your six-year-old daughter fixes you a small cake from her toy oven. Do we believe it's the right thing to rave about that cake? Absolutely. Do we believe it's the right thing to tell her she should really consider opening her own bakery to sell toy oven cakes? Of course not. Why? Because what your daughter needs to hear is that *you* love that cake. She needs you to focus on that moment, on that special gift she is giving you—not on some unrealistic tale about how the cake should be packaged and sold to the public.

It's that kind of focus that we need to carry into everyday life. When a colleague comes to you with a report that's flawed, tact requires that you kindly offer constructive criticism. You actually cheat your colleague when you offer a phrase like "I really like this. I think you'll do well in the meeting with this report. Don't change a thing."

Little white lies actually prove that we haven't given the situation at hand, or the people around us, the attention they deserve.

Tactic 11: Truth Doesn't Equal All-Out Attack

We've already discussed truth as a weapon. You can go back to chapter 2 if you want to review that discussion. This tactic calls us to use truth as a healing agent.

The challenge here is to position the truth to bring healing in every situation. This doesn't mean, as you should know well by now, that truth is painless. But it does mean that the truth should be applied specifically for the good of someone else.

A common example would probably work best here. Suppose you've hit middle age. You visit your doctor. During the appointment, your doctor turns to you and says, "You're too fat. You're lucky your blood pressure isn't off the charts. Lose weight or die, Mr. Toad."

All those things may be true. Yet those statements, as motivating as they might be, are presented in an attack mode rather than a healing mode. And for most patients, an approach that attacks might actually be less motivating than an approach that encourages. Everyone needs encouragement and hope now and then.

So what if the doctor tried to state his case this way: "You know, middle age hits everybody. Some of us are caught by surprise with what happens to our bodies. The good news is, weight loss isn't as hard as it looks. And the benefits it brings to your heart and overall health makes it well worth the effort. You need to make some changes, starting today, to lose some weight. It's time to pick your favorite sport, something you can do two or three times a week, while you cut back on unhealthy foods. I think we'll see good progress in pretty short order."

All these things are true, too. But it's clear that the goal of these statements is to heal, not to attack. And please remember this: healing statements aren't just for the doctor's office.

Tactic 12: Specify the Negative

In everyone's life, a time comes when we want to have a heart-to-heart talk with someone about his need to change. Sometimes in our enthusiasm to help someone, we forget our own need to prepare for the encounter.

Any time we offer correction to someone else, it's crucial that we be specific about what needs to be corrected. And why is this?

Remember the coach who told you, "You really need to work on your game," but neglected to tell you what part of your game you needed to work on? How about the supervisor who said, "I need to see better job performance out of you," yet overlooked telling you how you were supposed to make that happen?

How did you feel after those encounters? Ready to conquer the world, or ready to call it quits?

The best coach was the one who could tell you specifically that you needed to turn your toes inward to run a faster sprint. She was the one who went "inside the paint" with you to show you how to box out an opponent for a rebound. The best supervisor was the one who gave you the details about putting a report in better form or about getting along with the company vice president.

Sometimes this means we need to prepare a list, item by item, of the negative things we hope to confront in someone else. (Our memories aren't what they used to be, either.) The other advantage of getting a specific list together: If you can't be specific about what needs to be corrected, chances are you don't need the encounter at all. Then the problem lies not with the other person, but with your perception.

That's why this tactic is a crucial component of your game plan as you put this book's Rule of Truth into practice.

Tactic 13: Accentuate the Positive

Yes, we *did* borrow this tactic from an old song. And it works.

Truth is not always negative. In fact, there's a lot of good to be pointed out in almost every person and in most situations. However, it can be a profound discipline to point out the good.

Depending on who your reference is, common wisdom says that for every single negative comment you give someone it takes seven to ten positive comments to keep him feeling good about himself. From our own experience, it seems that you need at least two positive comments to one negative to keep the people around you encouraged about a difficult situation.

This tactic is crucial in circumstances that seem to be mostly negative. Without some basis to build a positive platform on, it's nearly impossible to take positive action. We're not suggesting that you become Pollyanna. But we do believe it's important in most cases that you help others recognize that a situation offers more hope than the post-iceberg *Titanic*. Why? Because that's the truth about most situations.

That being said, don't wait for a disaster to bring positive truth to bear on the circumstances and people around you.

Tactic 14: Truth Is Both Practice and Principle

If you got anything out of this book, we hope you understood the need to put truth into practice. Even though this book began as a conversation over coffee, we don't want to leave it there.

It's amazing that so many people from so many backgrounds agree that truth, in principle, is important to everyday life. It's just as stunning that so many of us who would go to the mat for the principle of truth ignore the everyday application of truth.

Practicing truth is a discipline. Like so many other disciplines, it requires scheduling. That scheduling is especially critical for those of us at work to restore integrity to everyday life. So here's our suggestion: Every day for the next twenty-one days, plan three occasions to tell the truth. Use the tactics listed above for ideas on how to tell the truth—maybe even where to tell the truth. To help in this process, we've included a workbook in the next chapter, which will assist you by giving you some places to begin your thinking and work.

Truth-telling requires a commitment and a plan of action. As the now-embedded advertising slogan from a popular athletic-wear company says, we need to "just do it."

Where Do You Go from Here?

Through these fourteen tactics, we hope you'll discover that truth-telling is not only important in principle, but possible—and crucial—to put into practice. It's not always easy or without cost, but truth-telling is the right thing to do.

It's one thing to tell stories of noble knights whose bold dedication to the truth was an expected part of their chivalrous behavior. Such heroes are often made into legends. Truth cost some of them their fortunes. Others practiced truth in a lifelong quest for nobility.

But the real heroes for today are those who will make it a point to restore truth into everyday life. These are the people who will tell the truth about their mistakes before their colleagues and children. They're the ones who will offer truthful correction to someone else, not to wound them, but rather to start that person on the path to wholeness. They are the everyday folks who are determined to bring honesty back to the marketplace and into the workplace. These are the people who are making it a point to confront the ethics of the exception so that truth might again become an everyday standard.

Perhaps you're one of them. The key here, of course, is that you start to work truth-telling into your everyday life—and you can use the tactics above and the exercises in the workbook section that follows to do just that.

All this being said, we wouldn't kid you: We don't imagine that anyone will become a knight in shining armor simply by telling the truth on a daily basis. But we do think, as time goes on, that you just might look more like one to your family, friends, and the people you work with.

the workbook: fourteen tactics for telling the truth the workbook: fourteen tactics for telling the truth the workbook: fourteen tactics for telling the truth the workbook: fourteen tactics for telling the truth the workbook: fourteen tactics for telling the truth the workbook: fourteen tactics for telling the truth the workbook: fourtee

Chapter

11 ▶ the workbook

fourteen tactics for telling the truth

While you've already encountered these tactics in chapter 10, you now have the opportunity to do some homework that will help you apply each tactic to everyday life.

You don't need to take on the tactics all at once. In fact, the best use of your time is to do a quick review of the tactics and pick out one or two that immediately grab your interest. The key challenge is to put them into practice. You choose the order.

Tactic 1: Understand the Power of Words

What You Need to Know

Language has limits. What you say—and what you don't say—affects the way the truth you want to tell is understood.

It boils down to the following three principles of language. They have been stated and restated by semanticists (people who study meaning in language) for about a century now. You may have heard of one or more of these principles, or variations thereof. But here's how *we're* stating them for your use, with brief explanations included:

1. The word is not the thing. This simply means that language is language, and not the reality it describes. You call the green stuff that makes up your lawn "grass." So do we. But the word "grass" on this page, or on our lips, isn't actually the green stuff that makes up your lawn. Why is this important to know? *When you tell the truth, you need to understand that your own words don't mean much without the reality to back them up.*

2. You can't say everything about anything. Do you remember the old phrase "the truth, the whole truth, and nothing but the truth"? There's a problem with saying "the whole truth." It's only the whole truth as best you can tell it. Take a six-year-old, an entomologist, and your Aunt Flossie to the backyard. Ask the question "What do you see?" The six-year-old will take note of the swing set, no doubt. The entomologist will check out the caterpillar on the third rosebush from the left. Aunt Flossie will compliment you on washing your patio furniture. And unless you prompt them to notice something else, chances are those are the memories—and therefore descriptions—of your backyard that each one will take with them. When they tell their stories about your backyard, they could all tell the truth, and each tell something entirely different. Why is this important to know? *Even in your best efforts to tell or hear the truth, you need to remember there's no way one observer can say everything about anything.*

3. You can end up talking about talking. One of the limitations of language is that you can say a whole lot about nothing. Imagine yourself in a vapor lock eating chocolate to the sound of shuffling cards. Look at that last sentence again. Did it do anything besides become a glaring example of this point? Enough said. Why is this important to know? *As you tell and hear the truth, remember that just because something is put into words doesn't necessarily mean it's significant.*

It all boils down to this: The very nature of language should be enough to humble the boldest truth-teller among us. It should serve to remind us that as perfect as our understanding may be, the way we express it will not be perfect.

Now, with these points in mind, let's see how they apply.

A Possibly Obvious Example

You want to tell the truth.

You're at home, ready to pull out the stops and let your daughter (or spouse or roommate or . . .) know that it's time to pick up after herself.

You begin with the word "Sophie," because that's her name. So far, so good. You move on with "The house is a mess, and most of it is *your* mess. Mess, mess, mess . . . and probably *mold* to go with it."

Sophie checks through the various piles in the family room where you both stand. No mold. Your last phrase is meaningless without the reality to back it up. Truth is being compromised.

Next you try "I see piles of your stuff all over this room." But Sophie, who has just put up a lovely mural on the family-room ceiling, says, "I see walls in desperate need of paint." You remember that both phrases can be true due to your different points of observation. You agree with Sophie, so in turn she reluctantly agrees with you.

Score! You enter into the realm of shared reality. You agree about the truth of the piles, which could lead you into an agreement about Sophie's need to deal with them.

You could parlay this into the coup de grace of the conversation if you handle the next sentence well. "So, Sophie, getting to the point: Please, I need you to pick up after yourself now." Sophie responds, "But Dad (or honey or buddy or . . .), many great artists live in clutter. In fact, the whole point of chaos in the Dada movement of the early twentieth century was to . . . "

Aha! Immediately you realize that Sophie is talking about talking to avoid the reality of the room! Although many use this as an artful dodge, you know that such behavior shouldn't be encouraged by practicing truth-tellers and truth-hearers.

"Sophie, let's not avoid the issue. I'll get you a laundry basket. Maybe a steam shovel."

Sophie begins the search for a steam shovel in the driveway. You forgot that you need reality to back up your words.

▶ Exercise! Practice!

So how can you begin to use language more accurately? How can you best avoid the pitfalls caused by the limitations of language?

Try the Description Game. You can do this on your own in four easy steps:

1. *Take a pad and pencil.*

2. *Pick a room (or a backyard, if you'd like).*

3. *Write down what you can see and describe in one minute.*

4. *Evaluate what you write. Here's what you should include in your evaluation:*

▶ Was what you wrote accurate? Do the reality check. Maybe the ink spot you thought you saw on the carpet was part of the pattern.

▶ How much did you miss? Try to notice a few things that you didn't have time to notice. It's just a reminder that your powers of observation are limited.

▶ Did you have time to be eloquent? If you let it, this exercise will help you communicate with less "fluff" in both written and spoken communication.

Try two or three rounds of the Description Game on your own, then bring someone else along into another room to try it with you. Check your answers against each other. Find out what kind of details other people notice that you miss and vice versa.

You can vary the game by trying to describe smells and sounds in addition to sights. In any case, use the game to help you discipline your words toward reality-based descriptions without much fluff.

▶ *And This Week . . .*

Plan what you're going to say in at least one conversation each day. We're not saying you have to strictly script your encounter with someone else, but think about these three points:

1. *Is there reality behind the words I'm saying?*

2. Do I realize no one can say everything about anything—and therefore, I should neither try to nor expect others to?

3. Am I cutting out extra words to make my conversation as accurate as possible?

Put the tactic into practice, and language will become your ally in being heard and understood as you tell the truth.

Tactic 2: If There's a Problem, Say So

What You Need to Know

You *can* talk constructively about problems. Saying nothing about a problem is usually another way of lying about it.

What kind of problem gets solved by ignoring it, anyway? We're sure such problems exist. Maybe they fall into the category of skin rashes you should try not to scratch. But even then, wouldn't you want some kind of medicated ointment to help?

Hmmm. Maybe that problem *doesn't* exist after all—except when we're to be the ones to call attention to it. That's right: even in the brave new world of the new millennium, we're too often "truth wimps" when it comes to letting someone know there's a problem with a situation.

To be sure, being the one to bring up a problem can put you on eggshells. It might even cause you to be singled out as a troublemaker for a while. But if the problem is real, and you say nothing—well, isn't that a lot like a lie? And when others realize the problem is real, too, won't the integrity of the situation improve?

That's why this tactic is so important in this age of political correctness and wanting everyone to feel good about themselves. *We still have to take the responsibility upon ourselves to tell the truth when we see a problem.* We don't need to make more of the problem than it is. But we must be sure that what begins as a small problem doesn't grow into a huge one—and that the huge problem doesn't become dangerous to the integrity of our home, workplace, or society.

A Possibly Obvious Example

In this book we hammered home (we hope) the notion that a supervisor owes it to those under her to be honest about problems in job performance. In the same way, employees have a responsibility, too.

Our friend Dave was a part-time counselor at a public clinic. As can be the case in such places, Dave found himself with too many clients for the hours he was scheduled to work. He came up for a performance review—and immediately found himself under fire for doing "quantity, not quality" work.

The problem was, Dave couldn't put in more hours by state law. And his supervisor had seen that Dave's clients did better in a shortened session than other counselors' clients did in longer sessions. So she had purposely assigned Dave what would have been an overload for the other counselors in the clinic. Dave's really good at what he does—and he wasn't about to let the "quantity, not quality" phrase go on his performance review without an explanation.

So Dave did the uncomfortable, thinking he could jeopardize his job. He said, "I have a problem with this evaluation."

His supervisor and the human resources representative in the room with him looked surprised. The supervisor took the lead. "Can you tell us about it?"

Dave nodded. "Absolutely. You've been overloading me on the number of clients I see because you know I can handle them, right?"

The supervisor nodded slowly.

"But the state says I can't work more hours to offer them more time, right?"

This time the human resources rep nodded.

"You have me in a double bind. I completely resent being made the victim of a structural problem. I won't sign the review until you amend it."

On the spot the supervisor, the human resources rep, and Dave worked on the wording of a revised review that they could all sign. Dave's willingness to say there was a problem paid off for him that day. It paid off for others, too, as it caused the clinic to rethink the ratio of clients to counselors.

So what do you do when you see a problem? Are you willing to address it forthrightly, or do you prefer to let things go *ad infinitum, ad nauseum* for the sake of your comfort?

We think *discomfort* is indeed the primary reason people don't want to talk about problems in a relationship or a situation. So to exercise your truth-telling "chops" in confronting a problem directly, let's play the Discomfort Game.

Following are three situations that tend to cause discomfort in most people, especially as they realize they have the responsibility to confront someone about the problem. Read through the situations below, answer the questions about the situation, and carefully develop the words you'd use for truth-telling. If you can do this exercise with someone else, all the better. Practice using your truth-telling responses on each other.

Situation 1: You're in a grocery store when you notice Ziggy, one of the neighborhood kids. You say hi to each other as you continue your shopping. A few moments later, as you approach the checkout stand, you see Ziggy slip something into his jacket pocket from the candy-bar shelf. You're not sure you believe your eyes, but you watch Ziggy hurry past the checkout rows to the gum machines in the entryway. He's still there when you're pushing your filled (and paid-for) cart out the door. You know you'd want someone to talk to your son if they saw him under similar circumstances, so . . .

1. What makes you uncomfortable in this situation?

2. What are the possible benefits of you taking the initiative to confront Ziggy with the truth?

3. What do you say to Ziggy in this situation to constructively address the problem?

Situation 2: Your friend Elvira, always the free spirit, has a certain penchant for standing out in the office. She tends to dress a little on the outlandish side for an accounting firm. She lets you in on the secret that she's scheduled today to get a tattoo on her left wrist. It's a "delicate rose pattern," as she describes it. Yet you've also been a participant in meetings where a trend has been clear: the firm partners will likely tighten the office dress code in the next few weeks.

1. What makes you uncomfortable in this situation?

2. What are the possible benefits of you taking the initiative to confront Elvira with the truth?

3. What do you say to Elvira in this situation to constructively address the problem?

Situation 3: Let's put you in the place of Dave, who you read about in the previous section. You're good at your job. Because you're good, your supervisor is loading you up with more work than most of your peers. When your job review comes up, you're criticized for pushing "quantity" work through without as much "quality" as you could. You feel the evaluation is unjust, and you certainly don't want it going into your record without some amendment.

1. What makes you uncomfortable in this situation?

2. What are the possible benefits of you taking the initiative to confront those who are evaluating you?

3. What do you say to your evaluators in this situation to constructively address the problem?

If you see a problem you need to address, do it. We're not suggesting that you look for a problem that doesn't exist. But if you know of something—or see something happen—that you can reasonably address, do it. And to prepare yourself, consider the same points you went through in the exercises above:

► What makes you uncomfortable in this situation?

► What are the possible benefits of *you* taking the initiative to confront the problem with the truth?

► What do you say in this situation to constructively address the problem?

Tactic 3: If There's Not a Problem, Say So

What You Need to Know

Proactive talking is crucial for keeping the truth clear. There are plenty of us who want to see trouble when no trouble is there. That makes it twice as important for those of us who see there is *no* trouble to make that known.

Because of the unhealthy ways we've learned to communicate, we set ourselves up for more problems than actually exist. Sometimes we follow the lead of communication patterns from people who aren't forthcoming about their feelings, perceptions, or attitudes. We perpetuate a communications vacuum, which often creates a sense of paranoia about people and situations.

Unfortunately, many of us intentionally use this vacuum to give us—or allow us to keep—power over others. This is popularly known as "the silent treatment." The unfortunate thing about the silent treatment is that we've become so two-faced in our communication styles that we often can't tell whether someone is being graciously quiet or punishing us with her silence. In most cases, punishment that comes in this form does so because the person has learned to *passively* tell you about something rather than having the courage to speak out straightforwardly.

"No problem" is usually good news, isn't it? Then it's news worth mentioning.

Whether you realize it or not, if someone else needs you to reassure her that there's no problem and you maintain the silent treatment, you're creating another problem. So do yourself, and the people around you, a big favor: if there's no problem between you and them, let them know.

A Possibly Obvious Example

Very few circumstances are as scary for a child as not knowing where he stands with a parent. But that was the way Eddie was growing up.

What made Eddie's situation all the more ironic was that his parents, Tess and Richard, were both successful family therapists. It seemed that when they came home from the office they shared, their time for listening and talking alike was gone. Eddie was growing up with not just quiet evenings at home, but sometimes even silent evenings.

There were some nights when one of his parents came home boiling from a rough day at the office. Eddie didn't know where the anger was coming from, so he frequently believed he was the cause of his parents' distress.

By the time Eddie was six, he was already acting up in school. He withdrew abnormally into himself when he wasn't doing something disturbing. After two rounds of reassuring themselves that Eddie was simply having a problem adjusting to school, the third notice from the principal was enough to gain his parents' attention.

So Tess and Richard started with a checklist. They had Eddie in the typical round of activities: tee ball, piano lessons, soccer. They made it to church pretty regularly and had taken some vacations worthy of professionals of their standing. What had they missed?

They called one of their most respected peers, Tony, to help. Tony came out of his first session with Eddie and motioned to Tess and Richard. He called back into his office, "Eddie, you can keep working with that modeling clay. Why don't you make me another spaceship? I'll be just a minute." Then he ushered Tess and Richard into a side room and shut the door.

"I need a quick and honest answer. Even though we're friends, this is still under the umbrella of professional confidence. What you say stays here. So tell me, are you two getting along?"

Richard was startled and looked at Tess. "Why, yes. At least I think so." Tess nodded her agreement.

"Is there anything on the home front that upsets you regularly? Finances, goals—I don't know, maybe even allergies?"

Tess shook her head in wonderment. Richard thought for a moment, then agreed.

"Is Eddie doing something to anger or frustrate you?"

Richard shook his head firmly. "No. He's a good kid."

"When was the last time you told him that? I mean, in those words?"

Tess and Richard had no answer.

"Let's try this: when was the last time you really talked about *Eddie's* day when you came home from work?"

There was silence for a moment. Then Tess answered, "Tony, we haven't done that at all."

"The only thing I really got out of Eddie this hour is this: 'Mom and Dad are mad at me, and I don't know why.'"

Richard was nearly in tears. "*That's* what he's picking up from us at home?"

Tony simply nodded. Then he offered a series of ideas. Tess and Richard would be sure to include Eddie in conversation around the dinner table. They would each take time to ask about his day and tell him something about theirs. They would be sure to tell him something positive about his behavior and how proud they were of him. The silent treatment in their household had been unintentional—and now it would be over.

It still took Eddie a few months to believe his parents weren't angry at him over something. But the message finally sank in—because they took the time to tell him so.

▶ Exercise! Practice!

This exercise is meant to help you determine if your habits make you more or less likely to be a proactive communicator—and to give you some ideas to help you become one, if you're not. We call it the Proactive Pretest. Rate yourself by placing a mark on each of the scales on page 138. Try to limit your responses to a single relationship (spouse, sibling, parent, coworker, and so on) or situation (work, church, the tennis club, home, and so on). Why? Because many of us have a different communication pattern for each relationship and environment.

Here goes! Do you tend to be more . . .

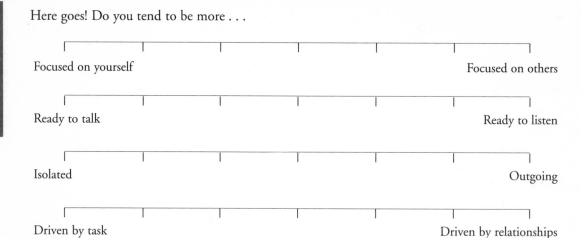

Focused on yourself — Focused on others

Ready to talk — Ready to listen

Isolated — Outgoing

Driven by task — Driven by relationships

Overscheduled — Able to give time to others

The more marks you made to the right, the more likely you are to be a proactive communicator. The more to the left, the more tendency you might have to give the silent treatment to others, even unintentionally.

So what can you do? Scoring to the left doesn't make you a bad person, but it might give you the indication that you need to practice more of the characteristics on the right in some settings to avoid giving others the silent treatment.

And why is the above just a pretest? Because the real test comes when you put the information into action.

▶ *And This Week . . .*

Take a hard look at your relationships and settings. If your silence might be causing someone to think there's a problem when there isn't, let that person know there's no problem. Consider working more toward the following characteristics from the exercise above:

▶ Focus more on others.
▶ Listen more to others.
▶ Be more outgoing.
▶ Work more on relationships than on your agenda.
▶ Try to spend more time on others.

The key here? Silent treatments, intentional or not, are usually given by those who focus more on themselves than on others. This doesn't mean you're inherently selfish. It can simply mean you're introverted. (Both of us are, and we had to learn extrovert skills to compensate. It *is* possible to become more outgoing through such strategies as intentionally starting conversations with someone else.)

In any case, be careful of the signals you *don't* send.

Tactic 4: Clarify, Don't Mollify

What You Need to Know

It's always tempting to dodge a difficult person or situation. If you can't "do the dodge," the next temptation is to try to talk your way around the problem to avoid hurting others' feelings—and your own status as the nicest person in the world.

Alright. Maybe, like us, you've already lost the "nicest person in the world" title. But you still need to practice this tactic. When you decide to take on the responsibility of telling the truth in a difficult situation, you're entering into one of the most delicate areas of truth-telling.

It's only human nature to desire to ease the burden for the sake of the people you're talking to. We still want you to be kind, but we don't want you to be so kind that you neutralize other people's need to recognize and act upon the truth you're telling.

And be clear about the problem. In these cases, it's usually best not to delve into a complicated history about why things are the way they are. It's much better to deal with the present, to help the party involved take appropriate responsibility for the needed correction, and to offer your encouragement toward that end.

A Possibly Obvious Example

A series of mergers left the corporate structure at Bobbie's company in shambles for a while. Employees everywhere were waiting, with great hope, for a revised structure to be implemented. The promise was that it would happen within six months.

As a department head, Bobbie knew—her other team members didn't—that her department was among many that were likely to be completely eliminated in the new structure. The people she'd been working with, some for nearly ten years, would be without jobs. So would she, but that didn't cause her as much inner anguish as thinking about the people she worked with.

Bobbie was wrestling with some options, none of which seemed very good at the moment. Should she call the team together and encourage them to start looking for other jobs? But what if there was even a slim chance that their department could survive? Should she let them enjoy their last few months as a team without adding the extra—and possibly needless—pressure of trying to buckle down to a higher standard of performance?

Bobbie knew that her department would stand a better chance of surviving the cut if they could demonstrate their competency. That would mean being accurate and timely with reports—two areas where her team did enough to get by, but not enough to achieve excellence.

Bobbie finally decided to lay it all on the line for her team. "I need to let you know that our department may not survive the cuts that will come with restructuring. There's no use in trying to revisit history; mergers happen and people lose jobs."

She let that news settle in for a moment. (But also notice here that she's not setting the conversation up for a long discussion about history, and she's clarifying the situation.) Then she continued. "If you decide you want to—and I hope you will—there are some things we can do that could help position our department to survive the cuts. That means, of course, we'd all still have jobs.

"I can't guarantee a thing. But I know our department is in competition with many others right now. It would be so easy for me just to say that all we have to do is keep on keeping on, but that's not the case. In fact, we have a problem with our reports. I can't help but think that if we did a better job with both the accuracy and the timeliness of our reports, and if the people upstairs could see how good we really are, that we'd stand a much better chance of making the transition into the new structure.

"I'd like to keep working together if we can. What do you say?"

Bobbie's team took on the challenge. Bobbie had done a great job of clarifying the situation, helping the team take responsibility for what needed correction, and encouraging the needed change. She had very little control over what would happen from there.

▶ **Exercise! Practice!**

Practice your clarifying skills—without mollifying—by working through the following three exercises, called Clearing It Up: Part 1.

Situation 1: Your son Jeff, usually a straight-A student, comes home with a C in math on his report card. He expresses dismay and confusion over the grade. You visit the teacher and find out that the issue is that your son isn't showing his work on his daily assignments. "Without that work, I have no idea what part of the process Jeff doesn't understand." And the teacher then shows you plenty of evidence that Jeff isn't understanding math from his assignments of the last quarter.

1. What would you say to help clarify the situation for Jeff?

2. How would you suggest that Jeff take proper responsibility for the needed correction? How can you help?

3. What will you say to encourage Jeff to take the appropriate action of correction?

Situation 2: Sid is one of the nicest people you know. He loves being part of the community theater. You get a call one night from the theater director with a favor to ask. "You know, Sid's as old as we are. This play calls for a young male lead, and Sid's talked himself into thinking that he's right for the role. Truth is, the Harris kid that just graduated from college is also part of the try-out, and it looks like *he's* got a lock on the part. Would you mind talking to Sid about it—let him know he's still great, but he might not be right for this part? I tried to broach the subject tonight, but just didn't get very far."

1. What would you say to help clarify the situation for Sid?

2. What would you suggest that Sid do to take responsibility for the needed correction? How can you help?

3. What will you say to encourage Sid to take the appropriate action of correction?

Situation 3: Your best friend's daughter—an honor-roll student and phenomenal musician—has announced to her parents that she wants to pursue medicine and not music as a career. She turns down a scholarship at a regional music school and enrolls in an honors program at the state university where she can pursue pre-med. You think her parents will be thrilled with their daughter's choice. But your best friend suddenly lets loose with a barrage of doubts over coffee one day, bemoaning the expense of all those music lessons over the years and worrying about how competitive medical school can be.

1. What would you say to help clarify the situation for your friend?

2. What would you suggest that your friend do to look again at her problem of perception? How can you help?

3. What will you say to encourage your friend to take the appropriate action of correction?

Speaking of friends: If you can, it could be helpful to do this exercise with a friend—or in a small group—and compare answers. You could also role-play the situations with each other.

▶ *And This Week . . .*

Prepare yourself to take on the responsibility to tell the truth in a difficult situation—and develop the strategies to clarify, not mollify. You can review the situations in the section above, or focus on a situation presently facing you. In any case, work on these points:

▶ Clarify the situation.
▶ Help the appropriate party take his responsibility in the situation.
▶ Encourage the appropriate action of correction—and don't make excuses as a means to avoid it.

What You Need to Know

There's another angle to consider when you clarify. Don't let your feelings surrounding a situation cloud the truth. Be sure that you deal with facts rather than opinions and emotions.

We need to be especially careful when our feelings may tend to paint someone else as a villain in a given situation. It can be tempting to make someone a scapegoat when things get tough. In our attempts to help someone accept the truth, it's easy to create an opening with that person by laying the blame for the situation with someone else.

The bottom line here? Truth is best served by clarifying who was responsible for inappropriate action. This isn't the place for a line like "The devil made me do it!" There may be underlying causes—causes that may even seem to be justified—for someone's action. But the situation is only clarified when those responsible for negative actions are individually confronted with *their* responsibility, others' actions notwithstanding.

A Possibly Obvious Example

Few things cause Colleen to fly off the handle. But listening to someone use spiritual language to elevate themselves above "the rest of us commoners" will do it.

It happened again at a basketball game. Colleen shuddered as she watched Cedric make his way toward her husband, Frank—but at least Frank was between her and Cedric.

Cedric didn't mind using spiritual lingo to let people know where he stood. "Hey, Frank, Colleen! Praise Jesus, it's great to see you!"

Frank dealt much better with Cedric than Colleen did. "Cedric! Good to see you! Why don't you sit down and join us?"

If Frank felt Colleen's elbow digging into his ribs, he didn't show it.

Cedric watched the game for, maybe, fifteen seconds before he started up. "Well, you know, I love basketball. I just wish there were some way to tie it in more directly to the work of the Lord."

Frank raised his eyebrows. Colleen just nodded and kept watching the game.

"I come here just to see who I can run into. Like you folks. Maybe it's a divine appointment that you're here. You know, I teach a wonderful Bible study. We do it on Thursday nights. Keeps our attention on the Lord and away from those worldly distractions on television."

Frank and Colleen groaned softly as they watched a referee miss an obvious foul call. Cedric noticed the call, too, and didn't let it go. "Hey ref! You need glasses or something? What ails you, anyway?"

People all around them turned to see who was making the racket. Cedric calmed down and continued as if nothing had happened.

"Yes sir, those worldly distractions—can't be too careful about them. They just sneak up on you and if you're not careful, you end up in the moral mud puddle just like the rest, . . . *Yo, Mr. Referee! Yeah, you! Can you count to three? Then call that three seconds in there, will ya?*"

Without taking a breath, Cedric continued. "So you see, if you don't want to end up like all these lost people around us here, you need some godly options in your life—like our Thursday night Bible study. Yep, bless God, praise Jesus . . . "

Colleen couldn't keep quiet anymore. She leaned across Frank and started in on Cedric—and didn't bother to take her voice down to a stage whisper. "Cedric, do us a favor here! If you have to use God-talk to prove your point with us, try a little mercy on the referee! And don't even start with your 'godly options' bit you're using to make yourself seem better than everyone else!"

The tongue-lashing had its desired effect. Cedric blushed a deep red, muttered a "See ya around" and moved to another section of the bleachers. The people immediately around Colleen applauded. "Way to go, lady!" "Thanks!"

But Colleen knew what was coming once the game was over. No sooner had she entered the car with Frank than he turned to her, speaking softly. "So when do you apologize to Cedric for publicly humiliating him?"

"But Frank, don't you think he deserved just a little humiliation?"

"Don't cloud the issue. We could have talked with Cedric away from other people. You enjoyed that way too much."

"I know, I know. And *I'm* responsible for *my* responses."

"Took the words right out of my mouth."

Sometimes truth-telling to a spouse is easy; sometimes it's not so easy—it depends on the relationship. But Frank knew Colleen was a person of great character, and he didn't want her to compromise that for a cheap shot taken at Cedric's expense. He called for Colleen to take responsibility for her actions, even though many in the crowd loved that she did what she did. He kept the issue clear and focused. It would have been easy to try to justify

Colleen's response based on Cedric's inappropriate behavior, but Frank didn't let that happen.

Practice your clarifying skills—without smearing—as you work your way through these Clearing It Up: Part 2 exercises.

Situation 1: There's no doubt about it: Trevor is one tough supervisor. In fact, he often resorts to insults as motivation to "coach" his team. After just a few months of employment with Trevor as his supervisor, Stan responded to a barrage from Trevor with a series of insults of his own. Trevor is ready to "write up" Stan, and Stan is ready to take Trevor's behavior to the human resources department. As one of Trevor's peers, you have his ear and could help the entire scenario.

1. What would you say to clarify the situation for Trevor without "smearing" Stan?

2. What would you say to clarify the situation for Stan without smearing Trevor?

3. What would you suggest to both Stan and Trevor to improve their working relationship? How would you state your case?

Situation 2: It's becoming apparent that Hilda, the new chairwoman of your book review club's membership committee, is completely incompetent in the role. Mailing lists have been misplaced, one-on-one encounters with potential members completely mishandled, and other committee members alienated. Irene makes it a point to make her opinion known through a poison-pen note that, while anonymous, makes no secret of who the author is. The club atmosphere is getting ugly, and you need to step in.

1. *What would you say to clarify the situation for Hilda without smearing Irene?*

2. *What would you say to clarify the situation for Irene without smearing Hilda?*

3. *What would you suggest to both Hilda and Irene to improve their working relationship? How would you state your case?*

Situation 3: "Keeping it simple" was never one of your brother Harry's strengths. So it's no wonder he's frustrating your son Sven as they work at starting a home-repair business together. Harry wants to improvise and jury-rig whenever possible. Sometimes he cuts corners in quality to try out one of his ideas. Often his improvising works, but the complexity he introduces to a work project costs a lot of time. Sven is more like you: not a great deal of imagination, but a hard worker who wants to do things right and efficiently. Finally, Harry calls you to say Sven blew up at him and he doesn't know why—except maybe this younger generation doesn't know how to work hard enough to make a living.

1. *What would you say to clarify the situation for Harry without smearing Sven?*

2. *What would you say to clarify the situation for Sven without smearing Harry?*

3. *What would you suggest to both Harry and Sven to improve their working relationship? How would you state your case?*

If you know of a situation where smearing might happen or is already happening, clarify it in a way that defuses the smearing. Taking cues from the above exercise, you can prepare yourself with three steps:

► Clarify the situation for the parties at odds.
► Demonstrate how to talk about parties within the situation without smearing them.
► Bring practical suggestions to parties within the situation to improve relationships.

Tactic 6: Give Credit Where It's Due

What You Need to Know

There's a fine art to giving an everyday, fact-based compliment. There's discipline involved in giving credit where credit is due, in communicating a specific fact about a job well done.

This tactic is the key to encouragement that matters. A child who hears a compliment based on a job well done—school work, chores at home, getting along with his sister—is on his way to repeating that positive behavior. A colleague who hears your gratitude for her part in making your job easier will feel better about you, your relationship, and likely the place where you both work.

And trust us on this one: giving your spouse a sincere, fact-based compliment for a good job on the home front can work wonders.

A Possibly Obvious Example

Terry and Tammy were as unusual a couple in their communication habits as you'd hope to find. It seemed, as opposite as they were in their patterns, that they fit together because they provided a good balance for each other.

It was rare for Terry to offer a compliment to anyone. Maybe that was because it was hard for him to receive one. "Just doing my job" was Terry's stock response to anyone's effort to commend him for his efforts. And that was the expectation he carried for everyone else: a compliment was always undeserved. Excellence, much less competence, was expected.

Tammy, on the other hand, was a "gusher." If your child did well in a piano recital, he was the next Mozart. If you had a successful term as an officer of a social club, you should run for Congress. Her exaggerations of others' accomplishments made people doubt her sincerity.

So how did Terry and Tammy learn the fine art of the fact-based compliment? Children. Terry found out that kids needed a verbal boost now and then. As their twins grew into their teenage years, Tammy found that they weren't taken in by exaggerated compliments—but that they'd love you forever for a well-placed, fact-centered piece of encouragement.

The lessons learned? Compliments were meant to be given freely—yet factually—where credit is due. And after a few years' practice with their children, Terry and Tammy were actually ready to hand out compliments to other people, too.

▶ Exercise! Practice!

Who can become your recipient for a fact-based compliment? Take time to make a Recipients' Report. Here's how: With plenty of space between the items, make a list of at least ten things you've done in the past twenty-four hours—driving your car, enjoying a meal at home, attending a meeting at work, and so forth. Then, in the space following each item, write the people it took to make these things possible (even pleasurable) for you.

For instance, if you write down "driving the car," you might list your mechanic, the car's manufacturer, and the cashier at your local gas station. Then suppose you wrote down "lunch at the local diner." You could list the waitress, the host, the cook, maybe the manager. Who organized that meeting at work that got right to the point and didn't waste anyone's time?

And remember to employ the fact-based compliment liberally at home. There are very few other truth-telling tactics that can build a child's sense of well-being as quickly—and compliments aren't bad for parents and spouses, either!

Hopefully, you'll have the opportunity and ability to offer a fact-based compliment to someone who helped make your day more positive. And once you get into the habit, you might make the fact-based compliment an everyday happening.

▶ *And This Week . . .*

You should be able to practice this tactic at least once a day for the whole week. Use your Recipients' Report to help you daily define your candidate for fact-based compliments. Remember, make your compliment a specific fact-based response to a job well done.

Tactic 7: Give Correction Where It's Due

What You Need to Know

As we mentioned in chapter 10, this may seem to repeat the "Clarify, Don't . . . " points (tactics 4 and 5). While there's a natural connection with these points, their application could be different. The points above are about *clearly confronting and assigning responsibility* in a difficult situation.

This point is about *offering correction.* It assumes that someone has a fairly clear, reality-based assessment of his role. The focus in this tactic turns to giving practical advice on the action(s) needed to make things better.

This should be fairly easy. As it is with giving credit where credit is due, giving correction involves the discipline of dealing with facts. So, one more time: Your role is to tie specific corrective action to the facts. Nothing more, nothing less.

This tactic is the key to giving—and receiving—advice that matters. Let it be a two-way street for you.

A Possibly Obvious Example

"Listen, I know Chicago like the back of my hand."

"Yeah. We all know, Ralph."

"So we take I-90 to the Eisenhower—that's 294—and then we'll get off at the Loop, go a back way to Washburn, and the restaurant should be three blocks on our left."

Ralph had made it clear he was the most qualified candidate for social director during the evenings of the sales conference that brought his team from Kansas City to the Windy City. What he didn't know was that Gene had grown up in Chicago. But Gene, being the quiet, reserved guy he was, wasn't about to compete for Ralph's role.

The team of four took their rental car off the exit ramp and followed Ralph's meticulous directions for the "back way" to Washburn. Trouble was, they suddenly found themselves facing cars coming at them in every lane.

They were headed the wrong way down a one-way, downtown Chicago street.

Gene cleared his throat. "Uh, I grew up just a couple of miles from here. Let's take a right between those two buildings—now."

They barely missed a taxicab, which had put on the brakes to avoid a head-on collision with them. Ralph was shaken up as much as anyone. "I'm sorry, I'm so sorry."

"Hey Ralph." Gene interrupted Ralph's nearly incoherent apology. "You got us most of the way here. Don't take it so hard. Can I get us back to the main path from this alley? I know where we are."

"Take it away, native son."

You'll notice that Gene didn't try to make Ralph look foolish. He didn't need to convince Ralph of his responsibility for the situation, either. Gene simply made the corrections that were needed. That's the key to this tactic.

► Exercise! Practice!

Try this exercise called Correction, Confronting, and Defining to work through your own strategy for giving correction where it's due. If you can do this exercise with a friend and review your answers together, all the better!

1. *How would you define the difference between correcting an error for someone and passing judgment on someone?*

2. *List three situations where you'd be willing to confront in order to correct an error (for example, giving directions to avoid a head-on collision, or stepping into a discussion to prevent false blame from being placed on a coworker):*

   a.

   b.

   c.

3. Define your own approach to confrontation with three descriptive words (for example, "gutless," "guileless," "bold," "reluctant"):

a.

b.

c.

4. In your own words, define the difference between "confrontation" and "attack."

5. What are some areas of knowledge where you'd feel comfortable offering correction if it was needed?

6. Is it easier or harder for you to make fact-based corrections? Why?

7. Are there any ongoing situations you're aware of that could use you as a corrective agent? If so, what are they?

If you know of a situation where you could be an effective and helpful agent of correction, take on the responsibility to be that. As always, don't invent one—just be ready with a fact-based correction where you see one is needed—especially if it helps someone dodge a head-on collision with reality.

Tactic 8: Talk to the Source of Your Problem

What You Need to Know

One of the most important tactics for telling the truth is dealing honestly with our problems. More often than not, this means we've got to speak honestly to ourselves. In other cases, it means we've got to speak honestly to the others who contribute to our problems.

Again, this tactic isn't about blaming someone else. This tactic is about doing what's needed to make a relationship better. A problem left unchecked can become a wedge between the best of friends.

Almost without exception, each of us will sometimes face the need to talk to someone else—perhaps even a friend—whose behavior has become our problem. To keep the relationship alive with that person, you'll need to talk to her about the problem behavior.

But never forget that for most of us, talking to the source of our problem begins by talking with the person staring back at us from the mirror.

A Possibly Obvious Example

It was a joy to have Roderick back in the house. He'd grown in a lot of ways from his summer as a camp counselor, and now he was staring down the pike toward his senior year of high school.

Jack knew he had a fine son. He really didn't like saying too much to correct him. Roderick never caused a problem to speak of. There was the occasional curfew correction, but even those were so rare that Jack couldn't remember the last one.

The problem was, Roderick's bedtime habits had changed significantly during his summer away. He stayed up later and made some serious racket as he went through his bedtime routine. It seemed as though Jack was hearing every detail of Roderick's regimen—and because Jack had to rise very early for work, the situation began to wear on him.

Jack couldn't wear earplugs because he wouldn't be able to hear the morning alarm, which he kept at a low volume to avoid disturbing his wife. But the two hours of sleep Jack was missing each night were beginning to take a toll on his energy. He knew he'd have to say something to Roderick.

He caught Roderick one evening right before dinner. "Son, I almost hate to bother you with this."

"What is it, Dad? What did I do?"

"It's almost incidental. This isn't an intentional thing on your part, so don't come down on yourself too hard. But it seems like ever since you've been home from working at camp, your bedtime regimen has gotten a lot louder. I hear everything you do, and since you're going to bed later—which is fine with me—I'm losing some sleep."

"Hey, Dad, let me see what I can do. Your beauty rest is really important to all of us, you know? I guess I haven't made the adjustment back to home from camp. You know, we had facilities away from the cabins, so the noise level wasn't quite as critical there as it is here. I'm sorry I've been keeping you awake. I'll work on it, okay?"

True to his word, Roderick made the adjustments necessary for a more quiet nighttime routine. Jack had talked to the source of his problem, however reluctantly, and achieved his goal.

▶ Exercise! Practice!

To check out your own need for truth-telling with this tactic, work through this Problem Source Analysis.

1. Describe one problem you currently face.

2. What's your responsibility in the problem?

3. Instead of looking at what you could have done differently before, describe what you can do now about the problem. (This is your contribution to the solution.)

4. Who must you go to in order to achieve a positive solution?

5. What might you have to go through to achieve a positive solution?

6. What will you say as you tell the truth to those who might be contributing to the problem?

7. What is preventing you from taking action to resolve this situation today? How soon can you bring the problem to a point of resolution?

▶ *And This Week . . .*

Schedule a time and take the opportunity to talk to the source of your problem, if such a situation exists for you. It can be easy to dodge the source of conflict—but wouldn't it be better to work out some kind of resolution that actually dealt with the problem?

Just remember that the goal of this tactic isn't simply to point a finger of blame at someone else, but rather to resolve an issue to build a better relationship.

Tactic 9: Recognize the Sources of Your Success

What You Need to Know

As we said in chapter 10, we believe that the self-made man—or the self-made woman—is a myth. One of the most important tactics for telling the truth, then, is to recognize the sources of your success. This tactic isn't an exercise in false humility. Rather, it's an honest recognition that others have contributed to the positive events in your life.

Sometimes it's tempting to keep all the credit for a personal success. Other times it can be just as tempting to turn down an honest compliment when you really deserve it. In either case, your personal integrity is compromised. You're not telling the truth, or perhaps not hearing the truth, about yourself.

One of the best things to do in such cases is to recognize the contributions of others. Let others know about the people who helped you along the way—and when you can, let those "helpers" know you appreciate them.

A Possibly Obvious Example

"Pete, congratulations! You won the production bonus this quarter!"

Pete had led his strategy team through some difficult maneuvering in the last fiscal year to streamline delivery time from the muffler plant to its distributors. It was a well-deserved reward. The bonus wasn't a fortune, but it would give Pete and his family a nice vacation.

Pete only entertained that thought for a few seconds, however. He went to the vice president over his division to ask a question.

"Hank, I wanted to stop by and thank you for the bonus."

"You deserved it, Pete."

"Thanks. Yet I was wondering if we could make out the reward certificate to my whole team."

Hank pursed his lips for a few moments, then nodded. "Sounds reasonable. Why?"

Pete smiled. "This was something that my whole team did. Everyone contributed ideas. We all went through the wringer together."

"Next thing you know, you'll be asking me to split the bonus check among your team."

"Well, now that you mention it. . . . "

Julie was one of Pete's team members. She had overheard that Pete was about to receive the production bonus. She came a few minutes early to the team meeting Pete had called that day. As the others made their way into the conference room, Julie tried to put the best face on Pete's good fortune for the rest of the team. "I heard Pete won the production bonus this quarter, guys. He did a great job leading our team, didn't he?"

Just then Pete walked in the door. He handed out a certificate and an envelope to every team member. "We won the production bonus this quarter! Congratulations!"

Hank walked through the conference room door right behind Pete. "This is the first time a team has won the bonus. Usually we single out one person, but Pete wouldn't let me do that this time around. You must really be something."

"They are, Hank. They are. I had to let you know about the sources of my success. They're all around the table."

▶ **Exercise! Practice!**

Do this Not-So-Secrets of My Success exercise as preparation to recognize those who have helped you along the way.

1. List three successes you've enjoyed in the past year.

   a.

   b.

   c.

2. What did you contribute to each of those successes?

3. Who else contributed to each of those successes?

4. How would your accomplishment(s) have been different without any one of the people who contributed?

5. Look at the list in question 3. Who from that list have you thanked and/or rewarded?

6. What might be an appropriate way to acknowledge those who have contributed to your success?

7. Who from the list could you acknowledge this week?

▶ *And This Week . . .*

Take the time to acknowledge—even if it's for the second or third time—someone who has contributed to your success. This should be a fact-based compliment, so be ready with specifics about how that person helped you.

Tactic 10: Tact Doesn't Equal Little White Lies

What You Need to Know

How do you let others know you disagree with them without hurting their feelings? Many of us choose not to let them know at all. Sometimes we keep silent. And other times we dodge a disagreement with verbal distractions.

These distractions are called "little white lies." Common wisdom says you tell these lies to prevent the greater evil of hurting someone's feelings. We believe tact calls for different tactics. Tact actually engages the truth with kindness. When required, tact even calls for constructive criticism.

Little white lies only demonstrate that we haven't given the situation at hand, or the people around us, the attention they deserve.

A Possibly Obvious Example

"Stuart, would you help me buy another car?"

It was the question Stuart had been hoping for in some ways. But now that the day was here, he looked at his mother-in-law, Sadie, with a sheepish grin and thought a moment before he answered.

What flashed through Stuart's mind in those moments? The trail of little white lies he'd left in the years he'd known Sadie. She was the grand mistress of finding and buying lemons. It didn't matter if it was new or used; it was as though Sadie's taste in cars was doomed to mechanical failure. She was usually taken in by the latest round of slick advertising. It didn't matter whether consumer and safety ratings completely trashed her choices; the ad campaign always won out.

Stuart was a nice guy. He really didn't want to make Sadie feel bad about her choices. That's why Stuart affirmed her even though everything he'd read and heard about a car she was choosing indicated she'd be better off buying a broken-down bicycle. When she bought the first-year model of a European gas miser that tended to fall apart quickly, Stuart said, "Mom, what a cute car!" When she bought the sports car famous for a worldwide transmission recall, Stuart said, "Mom, that'll really look good on the road!" When Sadie went through her sport-utility vehicle phase, Stuart affirmed, "That really looks like it will stand up to some tough terrain"—even though he knew her choice was rated "most likely to tip over" by three leading safety evaluations.

Okay, Sadie's feelings weren't the only consideration. Even more, Stuart didn't want to set himself up as an expert in Sadie's eyes by even beginning to give her advice. He knew that would put him in her decision-making loop when she bought a car, and he didn't want that bother.

But that was about to change. Stuart looked at Sadie and nodded. "Mom, I'd be happy to help you. But before we go visit a dealer, let me take you through the process I use when I'm shopping for cars. If I'd have done this with you before, you probably would have been able to make better choices."

You need to plan your words to avoid the trap of little white lies. Practice with three situations in the No More Little Whites exercise that follows.

Situation 1: Your friend Joe isn't exactly a natty dresser. His new tie is destined to prove that point. It looks like it belongs in the disco-leisure-suit-Spam era—and that's a kind analysis. Yet you like Joe. You really don't want to hurt his feelings. The problem is that Joe thinks the tie is perfect for his date with Natalie, who you know is particular about the way people dress.

1. What little white lie might you be tempted to tell Joe?

2. How would that little white lie possibly damage Joe instead of help him?

3. What will you tell Joe instead of a little white lie?

Situation 2: Tim's dog looks like a cross between Winston Churchill and a lizard. It's nearly as talented as a brick, but Tim loves it. In fact, he's about to sink major money into obedience school and grooming because he's convinced the dog can be prepared for an upcoming show and take the grand prize there.

1. What little white lie might you be tempted to tell Tim?

2. How would that little white lie possibly damage Tim instead of help him?

3. What will you tell Tim instead of a little white lie?

Situation 3: You, as an ever-imaginative entrepreneur, think you have the ultimate idea for a new best-selling product. You draw up the design and show it to your good friends Thomas, an outstanding engineer, and Donald, an amazing marketer. You would hope their responses would be truthful.

1. What little white lies might your friends be tempted to tell you?

2. How would those little white lies possibly damage instead of help you?

3. If they have "tough truths" to tell you, what do you hope your friends will say to you — and how do you hope they'll say it?

▶ *And This Week . . .*

If you've been engaging in little white lies, do your homework and start truth-telling. Remember that little white lies usually indicate one's lack of genuine interest in another person or situation. So this time through, consider the damage that little white lies might be causing others — and tell the truth with kindness. (See the next tactic for more on kindness.)

Tactic 11: Truth Doesn't Equal All-Out Attack

What You Need to Know

This tactic calls us to use truth as a healing agent in every situation. This doesn't mean, as we've pointed out several times, that truth is painless. But it does mean that the truth should be applied specifically for the good of someone else.

As motivating as some statements might seem at first, it usually demotivates listeners to hear them in an attack mode rather than a healing mode. So remember to speak the truth with the goal of healing.

A Possibly Obvious Example

"I've never seen a car in such horrible shape!" Lefty was nothing if not an honest mechanic. But that didn't make his words any easier for Laura to hear. She cringed as she waited for the next remark.

"There's enough grease on this engine to do a year's worth of French fries." Lefty chuckled at his own joke. "Someone must have been planning a second career in fast food . . . unless they were thinking about becoming a pig farmer. Look at that pig sty someone's using for an interior!"

Laura lowered her head and stared at the ground. As a college student, she rarely took the time to clean out her car between semester breaks.

"Too bad there isn't a Humane Society for cars—this one would be a prime example of abuse. The oil must be five thousand miles overdue for a change. There's gum in this crankcase instead of 10W-30!"

Laura had just learned how to check the oil. That's how she knew she needed to bring the car to a mechanic in the first place. But apparently she hadn't learned soon enough.

Someone touched her on the shoulder. "First car, miss?"

Laura turned to read the name "Chaz" on the name patch another mechanic was wearing. "Yes, it's my first car. And I feel like a complete idiot for even owning it right now."

"You don't have to. Lefty doesn't know how to talk without shredding something. That's his problem, not yours. Look, do you know how to check the oil?"

Laura nodded.

"Do your warning lights work?"

Laura nodded again.

"Once we do this oil change and tune up, you'll be able to drive it for three thousand miles unless you see a warning light or something exceptional like smoke under the hood. You need to watch your tire tread, and I'll show you how to check the fluid levels for your windshield solution and engine coolant before you leave. Then you'll never have to be in this situation again, okay?"

"Okay." Laura had almost told Lefty she'd be taking her business elsewhere. But Chaz was actually helping her do something constructive for her car—and for how she felt about herself. She'd be back.

▶ Exercise! Practice!

There are ways you can use the truth to hurt someone, of course. Putdowns will discourage almost anyone ("That's the poorest excuse for a birdhouse I've ever seen a Cub Scout build, son" or "You stink as a next-door neighbor" are just two examples). But the truth deserves better. Practice using the truth as a healing agent as you do the Hurt or Heal? exercise that follows.

1. You need to tell your child to bring her grades up. How might you tell the truth so it

hurts?

heals?

2. You need to tell a coworker that you believe his job is at risk. How might you tell the truth so it

hurts?

heals?

3. You need to tell your spouse that she has offended someone. How might you tell the truth so it

hurts?

heals?

4. *You need to tell a friend at church that he needs to stay awake during the pastor's sermon. How might you tell the truth so it*

    hurts?

    heals?

5. *You need to tell your sister that she needs a more stable employment record. How might you tell the truth so it*

    hurts?

    heals?

6. *Which type of statement above was easier for you to develop: those that hurt or those that heal? Why?*

    Of course, we'd suggest that you use the healing statements in everyday life.

► *And This Week . . .*

Is there one specific instance right now where truth will bring healing? If so, take on your responsibility to be a truth-teller. Remember, you have to think about truth's healing impact to avoid making it a weapon.

Tactic 12: Specify the Negative

What You Need to Know

In everyone's life, a time comes when you want to have a heart-to-heart talk with someone about his need to change. But sometimes in your enthusiasm to help someone, you forget your need to prepare for the encounter.

Any time we offer correction to someone else, it's crucial that we be specific about what needs to be corrected. Sometimes this means we need to prepare a list, item by item, of the negative things we hope to confront in someone else. If you can't be specific about what needs to be corrected, chances are you don't need the encounter at all. Then the problem lies not with the other person, but with your perception.

A Possibly Obvious Example

It was the fifth week of the painting class at the community college, and Delia was convinced it had been a monumental waste of time. For four weeks, she had endured the comments of a local artist whose only evaluation of her work had been "It's not quite right."

"*What's* 'not quite right'?" Delia had asked time and again. But all she received in response was an occasional "Hmmm . . . " before the artist walked away.

If she hadn't paid so much for the supplies, Delia wouldn't have bothered coming back to the class after the second week. At least the class gave her ninety minutes to work on her painting, she reasoned.

The advantage of this fifth week's class was walking through the door. "Hi, I'm Jessie, and I'll be teaching the class tonight."

Jessie demonstrated a few techniques with a brush, palette, and canvas to begin the class. Then she came around and offered hints to each student. Delia was overwhelmed when Jessie actually gave her suggestions to improve her painting style. "Now, let's try turning your brush a little more to the side. . . . Okay, for that color in this section, don't load your brush with too much paint. . . . Now in this part of your picture, you'll probably want to use a smaller brush."

Delia felt like the whole course had just been justified thanks to Jessie's specific help. She'd certainly made more progress on her painting that night than she had in the other four weeks combined.

Develop your ability to be more specific as you offer correction by working through the Your Specifics, Please! exercise that follows. Each question offers a situation and a too-general comment that says something negative without being specific. Your task is to add specifics (you may use your imagination as long as you're specific) to clarify the too-general comment. Here's an example:

The Situation: You're commenting on a friend's inability to stay in a meaningful relationship.

The Too-General Comment: "You sure can pick 'em, can't you?"

Your Specifics, Please (Here, list specific things that actually clarify the situation): "It seems to me that you need to take more time to get to know someone before you start a serious relationship. . . . You should make sure you share several common interests with anyone you think you want to be with for a lifetime. . . . The last three breakups you've had all happened right after you met the parents—it could be that makes you feel too committed—so are you ready to launch into another relationship if you're not ready to commit to it?"

Now try it yourself.

1. *The Situation:* You're a coach working with a (choose your favorite sport here) team that is behind halfway through the game (or match).

   The Too-General Comment: "Aw, we've got to change the whole way we're playing!"

   Your Specifics, Please:

2. *The Situation:* You're a parent commenting on a daughter's mode of dress.

   The Too-General Comment: "You're dressed like a tramp!"

   Your Specifics, Please:

3. *The Situation:* You're a supervisor conducting a job review with an employee.

   The Too-General Comment: "Overall, we'll have to see some improvement here, or you'll be written up."

   Your Specifics, Please:

4. *The Situation:* You're the lookout for the Titanic.

   The Too-General Comment: "Uh, there's something in the water ahead of us."

   Your Specifics, Please:

▶ *And This Week . . .*

If you need to offer any correction, be sure to make it specific correction. There are few things more frustrating than having someone say something's wrong and then walk away without letting you know *what* is wrong.

Tactic 13: Accentuate the Positive

What You Need to Know

Like the old song indicates, there's a lot of good to be pointed out—and truthfully so—in almost every person and situation. Focusing on that good point can be another matter, of course.

Here's a ratio that haunts us: Common wisdom indicates that for every single negative comment you give someone it takes seven to ten positive comments to keep them feeling good about themselves. As we mentioned in chapter 10, our own experience indicates that you need at least a two-positive-to-one-negative comment ratio to keep the people around you encouraged about a difficult situation.

The crucial element that will make this tactic successful is *hope.* You need to build a positive platform to launch positive action. That means you need to be ready to help others find points of hope even in situations that seem mostly negative.

A Possibly Obvious Example

The Stone family had performed as expected that morning and left for their vacation two hours late. This fact alone would not have been a problem, except Corean Stone had made reservations at a dinner theater in the city where they were supposed to stay that evening. It would be a tense day as a result.

The fact that it started raining didn't help. The fact that the rain became part of a near-monsoon made it even worse. So much for making up any time on the drive. Still, with no further delays, they'd have time to make it to their hotel for a quick cleanup and still make it to the dinner theater.

Raymond Stone was making occasional comments about that fact, trying to help the family keep a positive attitude about the day. That's when they all heard the *boom-flop-flap-flop* signaling a flat tire. Raymond pulled the car to the shoulder of the road.

There they were, in some serious rain and under the schedule's gun with a flat tire. Corean simply buried her head in her hands. Raymond helped the family take stock of the situation. "We could give up trying to make the dinner theater now. But instead, I'd like to remind you all that we have Jimmy Stone, a recent 'A' student from the Mayfield High auto mechanics class, in our midst. His younger brother Denny helped me double check the safety features of our station wagon. Therefore, he knows exactly where the tire iron and jack are. Under the umbrella I'll be holding, Jimmy and Denny will work to get us back on the road safely and in record time. Ready, gentlemen?"

The boys grinned at the thought of acting like a pit crew in a rainstorm. "Let's go!" Raymond grabbed Corean's umbrella and popped the tailgate on the station wagon so they could begin the process. Within a few minutes, the Stone family teamwork had conquered the flat-tire problem. Raymond, Jimmy, and Denny were drenched but safe in the car with the flat lashed to the roof.

They drove out of the rain in less than five minutes. Denny looked to the side of the car and whistled. "Will you look at that?" There, for their enjoyment, was a double rainbow.

The Stone family made the *other* show on time that day, too.

► **Exercise! Practice!**

Sometimes it helps to review the strengths of the people around you. Toward that end, it's a good idea to develop an Applause Book.

The point of this book is to honestly assess the good points of your family, your coworkers, and even yourself. Start with a small notebook. Write a person's name on each page. Under each name, write something good about that person. Perhaps she has a character trait you admire. Maybe you have a specific reason to be thankful for that person. It could be that she has a skill that you believe is an asset to others. You might not be able to come up with many things about some people—and that's okay. (Try the exercise with your own name at the top of the page, too.)

This can be a helpful exercise to do as a family, a work team, or a small group. In those settings, you could ask each person to add to the list under each of the others' names. When you're done, consider retyping the entries and offering each person his page as a gift of affirmation.

Whether you do this alone or with others, try to keep the strengths you've listed for the people around you—and yourself—in mind as you face a difficult situation.

► *And This Week. . .*

Find at least one situation where you can accentuate the positive to benefit those who may feel discouraged. Remember, we're about truth-telling here. Don't make up a bunch of blue-sky platitudes. Rather, give them an honest listing of the strengths they bring to the situation.

Tactic 14: Truth Is Both Practice and Principle

What You Need to Know

It's amazing that so many people from so many backgrounds agree that truth, in principle, is important to everyday life. It's just as stunning that so many of us who would go to the mat for the principle of truth ignore the everyday application of truth.

Practicing truth is a discipline. Like so many other disciplines, it requires scheduling. Truth-telling requires a commitment and a plan of action. As the slogan says, we need to "just do it."

A Possibly Obvious Example

The phone rang in the middle of the evening. When Roger went to check the caller ID box, he noticed the dreaded word "Unavailable." That meant it was either his mother-in-law or a telemarketer. Given the time of day, it was likely a telemarketer. Roger sighed as he picked up the phone.

"May I speak to Mr. *Smighth?*"

"That's 'Smith,' ma'am. And you're speaking to him."

The conversation went as might be expected. Roger knew he didn't want another mortgage on the house, so he found a way to excise himself from the conversation after only a minute or two.

But Brian, Roger's ten-year-old, had listened with great interest. "Dad, why didn't you just pretend to be someone else and tell them you weren't here?"

"Because that wasn't the truth, son. Have you known me to dodge the truth any other time?"

Brian thought for a moment, then shook his head. "I can't remember any."

"That's because I try to tell the truth every time I can. I don't always succeed the way I'd like to, but I try. Brian, I expect the same from you.

"Now, where's the number your mom copied down for that call-screening service they've been advertising on the radio?"

▶ Exercise! Practice!

Develop your own Truth Scheduler as a means to put truth into practice. Here's our suggestion: Every day for the next twenty-one days, plan three occasions to tell the truth. Use the other thirteen tactics listed for ideas on how to tell the truth—maybe even where to tell the truth.

You can use this chart or one you develop on your own. The row across the top offers four areas where you can tell the truth—in your family, at work, to yourself, or "other." (We're really flexible.) We encourage you to write both an approximate time and a word or two in the spaces that will help trigger the truth-telling event you've scheduled.

DAY	FAMILY	WORK	SELF	OTHER
Sample	*7 A.M.—Breakfast—Encourage Jack on math progress*	*10:30 A.M.—Jim—Timeliness corrective re: evaluations*	*Noon—Look in mirror—Salad, not a double cheeseburger*	*7 P.M.—Civic Club—Turn down chair—no time for family stuff*
1				
2				
3				
4				
5				
6				
7				
8				
9				
10				
11				
12				
13				
14				
15				
16				
17				
18				
19				
20				
21				

▶ *And This Week . . .*

Start using the scheduler to work intentional truth-telling into your everyday habits. But don't limit yourself to the scheduler. Through these fourteen tactics, we hope you'll discover that truth-telling is not only important in principle, but also not so tough to put into practice. Use this book as a reference—and encouragement—for your task.

Happy truth-telling!

► Notes

Chapter 1: The Role of Truth

1. Paul Copan, *True for You, but Not for Me* (Minneapolis, Minn.: Bethany, 1998), p. 24.
2. As quoted in *Peter's Quotations: Ideas for Our Time* (New York: Bantam, 1980), p. 501.
3. The Barna Research Group, *Donor Compass Baseline 1998,* Ventura, Calif., February–April 1998.
4. The Barna Research Group, *Omnipoll 1-94,* Ventura, Calif., January 1994.
5. Grace Slick with Andrea Cagan, *Somebody to Love: A Rock and Roll Memoir* (New York: Warner Books, 1998), p. 360.
6. Sissela Bok, *Lying: Moral Choice in Public and Private Life* (New York: Vintage Books, 1989), footnote, p. 31.

Chapter 2: The Rule of Truth

1. Paul Guay and Stephen Mazur, writers, *Liar, Liar,* A Brian Grazer Production, Universal City Studios, 1997.
2. *New York Times,* June 9, 1958.
3. The Barna Research Group, *OmniPoll 1-97,* Ventura, Calif., January 1997.

Chapter 3: The Impact of Truth

1. The Barna Research Group, *Omnipoll 2-93,* Ventura, Calif., February 1993.
2. Lyrics from the song "An Apology" by Hangnail (1999) courtesy of BEC Recordings, © Spinning Audio Vortex (BMI), www.becrecordings.com.

Chapter 4: Truth and Spirituality

1. The Barna Research Group, *Teens 1995,* table 53b, Ventura, Calif., January 1995.
2. The Barna Research Group, *Omnipoll 1-92,* table 50b, Ventura, Calif., January 1992.
3. From *The Matrix,* A Silver Pictures Production, Warner Brothers, 1999.
4. The Barna Research Group, *Omnipoll 2-93,* table 71b, Ventura, Calif., February 1993.

Chapter 5: The Response to Truth

1. This is an adaptation of a story offered in the training curriculum of the Universal Kempo Karate Schools Association. Many thanks to Chief Instructor Garland Johnson, a master storyteller in his own right.
2. The Barna Research Group, *Omnipoll 1-91,* Ventura, Calif., January 1991.

Chapter 6: Truth in the Family

1. Alexander Dru, ed. and trans., *The Journals of Søren Kierkegaard: A Selection,* no. 1395, (London: Oxford University Press, 1951), pp. 542-543.

Chapter 7: Truth in the Workplace

1. The Barna Research Group, *Omnipoll 1-95,* table 27a, Ventura, Calif., January 1995.
2. Joe Jackson, *A Cure for Gravity* (New York: PublicAffairs, 1999), pp. 131-132.

Chapter 8: Truth in Society

1. The Barna Research Group, *Omnipoll 1-97,* table 14a, Ventura, Calif., January 1997.
2. Barna, *Omnipoll 1-97,* table 13b.
3. Thanks to T-Bone Burnett for introducing us to this catchy concept.
4. Antonin Artaud, quoted in Susan Sontag, ed., *Selected Writings,* pt. 33, (Berkeley, Calif.: University of California Press, 1988), p. 485.

Chapter 9: The Truth: Sooner Rather than Later

1. The Barna Research Group, *Teens 1995,* table 53a, Ventura, Calif., January 1995.
2. Barna, *Teens 1995,* table 53c.
3. Barna, *Teens 1995,* table 53b.
4. Barna, *Teens 1995,* table 58.
5. Barna, *Teens 1995,* table 84a.
6. Barna, *Teens 1995,* table 84b.
7. Barna, *Teens 1995,* table 84a.
8. Barna, *Teens 1995,* table 86a.
9. Barna, *Teens 1995,* table 86b.
10. Barna, *Teens 1995,* table 95a.
11. Barna, *Teens 1995,* table 95b.

▶ About the Authors

Devlin Donaldson

Devlin Donaldson attended Judson College in Elgin, Illinois, where he majored in human relations with a minor in philosophy and religion. He received an M.A. in counseling psychology from Trinity Evangelical Divinity School in Deerfield, Illinois.

Devlin spent eighteen years with Compassion International, a Christian child-development organization that sponsors over 300,000 children around the world. His most recent position with Compassion International was director of marketing and development. In July of 1999, Devlin began work with TouchPoint Solutions, a consulting firm focused on helping non-profit organizations build efficient and effective major gift programs.

Devlin is the author of *How to Be a Great Boss Without Being Bossy* (Oliver Nelson). He has also written more than 1,000 album and book reviews.

Devlin has been married to his wife, Carol, for nineteen years. They have one child, Maria, and are in the process of adopting their second child. They live in Colorado Springs, Colorado.

Steve Wamberg

Steve Wamberg received a bachelor's of science degree in communication from Wayne State College in Wayne, Nebraska. After working as a musician and a graduate teaching fellow, he earned a master's of divinity degree with an emphasis in theology and ethics from Northern Baptist Theological Seminary in Lombard, Illinois.

In 1980, Steve and his wife, Annie, cofounded Harvesthome Productions, a not-for-profit church renewal ministry. At that time he also began writing professionally for ad agencies, curriculum publishers, and venture capitalists. In 1992, Steve accepted a position in the communication department for Compassion International, a Christian child-development agency. In April 1997,

Steve and Annie launched The Wamberg Group, Inc., to handle a growing demand for their consulting and writing services for mainstream businesses and not-for-profit agencies.

Steve has collaborated on a number of books. He is coauthor of *Making God's Word Stick* with Emmett Cooper (Thomas Nelson) and *Faith Teaching* and *Faith Parenting* with John Conaway (both Cook Communications). He has also written book reviews, hundreds of curriculum pieces (many with Annie), scores of print and radio advertisements, and regional music jingles. Steve and Annie have two children, Ben and Maggie.

STAND UP FOR YOURSELF AND YOUR BELIEFS.

Why Marriage Matters

Labeled old-fashioned and unnecessary, marriage is being abandoned for living together, single parenting, and sexual freedom. Based on one hundred years of social science research, this book gives us reasons to believe in marriage, even in a society characterized by a lack of commitment.

Why Marriage Matters (Glenn T. Stanton) $14

Who's to Blame

If you're tired of being hurt by the hurting people in your life, this book will give you the handle you need on the dynamics of victimization and blame.

Who's to Blame (Carmen Renee Berry and Mark W. Baker) $14

Get your copies today at your local bookstore, or call (800) 366-7788 and ask for offer **#6137**.

Prices subject to change.